The Beastly BATTLES of Old England

The Beastly BATTLES of Old England

The misguided manoeuvres of the British at war

NIGEL CAWTHORNE

piatkus

PIATKUS

First published in Great Britain in 2011 by Piatkus

Copyright © 2011 Nigel Cawthorne

The moral right of the author has been asserted.

A CIP catalogue record for this book
is available from the British Library.

ISBN 978-0-7499-5619-6

Typeset in Adobe Garamond by Phoenix Photosetting Ltd, Chatham
Printed and bound by CPI Group (UK) Ltd, Croydon, CR0 4YY

Papers used by Piatkus are from well-managed forests
and other responsible sources.

MIX
Paper from
responsible sources
FSC
www.fsc.org   FSC® C104740

Contents

Introduction	1
Chapter One – Ill-Advised Actions	5
Chapter Two – Ludicrous Leaders	37
Chapter Three – Misguided Manoeuvres	83
Chapter Four – Underestimating the Enemy	105
Chapter Five – Crazy Campaigns	123
Chapter Six – Fearless Foes	151
Chapter Seven – Misguided Gallantry	163
Chapter Eight – Ridiculous Retreats	181
Chapter Nine – Naval Nonsense	199
Chapter Ten – Aerial Engagements	239
Chapter Eleven – Uniformed Failures	251
Chapter Twelve – Suspect Supplies	261

Introduction

I APOLOGISE. THIS BOOK IS FULL of killing and death. But you knew that, didn't you? The title is *Beastly Battles of Old England*. It is a sister volume to *Strange Laws of Old England* and *Curious Cures of Old England*. They, too, contain a certain amount of killing – through both judicial and medical malpractice. The other book in the series is *Sex Secrets of Old England*. Not much killing there, hopefully. These books are supposed to be light and humorous. That means, of course, most of the humour in this volume is necessarily the darkest shade of black, if you will excuse the tautology – or is it an oxymoron? I can't decide.

Throughout history the English have been a warlike lot, so there have been plenty of battles. Often we fight among ourselves. There have been a good few civil wars. When we were not slaughtering each other, we practised on our neighbours – the Scots, the Irish, the Welsh, the Vikings, the French. And, when that got too easy, we set off around the world to find other people to fight. This was usually

1

done with a hubris that invited some ludicrous pratfall. But the occasional victory led to one small nation establishing the greatest empire the world has ever seen. How absurd was *that*?

Of course, battles, by their very nature, are beastly. People get killed, after all. But the English went into these conflicts, our enemies noted, as if they were playing some sort of sport. At the Battle of Tanga in East Africa in 1914, a victorious German said, 'You English are really quite incomprehensible. You regard war as a game.'

Even the Duke of Wellington noted, 'The Battle of Waterloo was won on the playing fields of Eton.'

What was particularly beastly about the Battle of Waterloo – apart from the fifty thousand casualties – was that it was a grudge match. While Napoleon had been in exile on Elba, *Monsieur le Duc* had been searching Paris for Boney's mistresses and sleeping with them.

British battles have also provided some wonderful moments of *sangfroid*. At the Battle of Waterloo in 1815, one of the last cannon shots of the day hit Lord Uxbridge.

'By God, sir, I've lost my leg,' he exclaimed. Wellington looked down and replied, 'By God, sir, so you have.'

More beastliness occurred after the battle. Teeth were harvested from the corpses left on the battlefield. These were used to make dentures and as transplants that were known as 'Waterloo teeth'.

Even the most dire defeat can produce odd ironies. Watching the Charge of the Light Brigade during the Crimean war, the French observer General Bosquet said famously, '*C'est magnifique, mais ce n'est pas la guerre*' – 'It is magnificent, but it is not war.' The English have always patted themselves on the back, assuming this was a compliment to their gallantry. However, what Bosquet really said was: '*C'est magnifique, mais ce n'est pas la guerre. C'est de la folie*' – adding 'It is madness' to show what he really thought. The English, it seems, could not take war seriously.

We British love a good war. In all the years that I have been alive, the British Army has always been in action somewhere around the world. Not that there is anything funny about young men and women fighting and dying. But, traditionally, the troops have used gallows humour to keep themselves going. And nothing changes. Throughout British history there have been a large number of expeditions that should never have been undertaken. They were doomed from the start, but went ahead out of ambition or

3

ineptitude. After all, God is an Englishman. What could go wrong? Well, just about everything. Even our first invasion of Afghanistan was a disaster. The second and third weren't much better. Some people never learn – though, I suppose, the military thinking is, we are bound to get it right sooner or later.

As a result, *Beastly Battles of Old England* is a cabinet of curiosities, a cornucopia of insufferable arrogance, reckless gallantry, stunning stupidity, massive misjudgements and general beastliness. Enjoy.

CHAPTER ONE

Ill-Advised Actions

 S WELL AS BEING BEASTLY, British battles are often balls-ups, fought for incomprehensible reasons by men who should have known better. Even the weather can be against you.

The way the wind is blowing

The Battle of Towton, Yorkshire, in March 1461 was conducted in a blizzard with disastrous consequences for the Lancastrians, who had fielded 42,000 against the Yorkists' 36,000. The Lancastrians also occupied the high ground, so they should have had the advantage. However, visibility was bad. The wind was blowing snow in their faces and aided the Yorkist archers, carrying their arrows further. After they had unleashed a volley into the Lancastrian ranks, they could easily fall back out of range of the Lancastrian archers, then advance again to pick up the enemy arrows that had fallen short.

The close-quarters fighting was so bloodthirsty that,

several times, the two sides had to stop and clear the bodies out of the way so that the front lines could get at each other. After ten hours, the Lancastrians found themselves outnumbered and outflanked. They were pushed back over the River Cock; it was said you could walk across the river on the bodies.

In the rout, many men dropped their weapons and flung off their helmets so they could breathe more easily as they ran. They were cut down. Several bridges collapsed under the weight of fleeing men, dumping them in the freezing water. Those who made a stand at Tadcaster were also butchered. It was the bloodiest battle of the War of the Roses.

The Lancastrian King Henry VI fled to Scotland, while those Lancastrian lords who had survived the battle tried to make peace with the Yorkist Edward IV. But that was by no means the end of it.

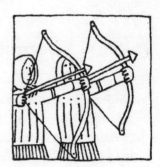

The fog of war

By 1470, the Earl of Warwick – 'The Kingmaker' who had started the War of the Roses in the first place by deposing Henry VI and putting Edward's father on the throne – had changed sides again and restored Henry to the throne. But, in March 1471, Edward returned from France with an army and, at 4 a.m. on 14 April, battle was joined at Barnet, just north of London.

It was a foggy morning and the two armies were slightly displaced laterally. This allowed the Lancastrian right wing, under the Earl of Oxford, to turn on the Yorkist left and chase them from the battlefield. When Oxford returned, through the fog, Warwick's men mistook his 'star with rays' badge for the 'sun in splendour' emblem of Edward, and attacked them. In the confusion, the battle was lost. Warwick, who was fighting on foot to avert the suspicion that he might change sides again and desert his men, was killed while fleeing – a victim of what the great nineteenth-century military theorist Carl von Clausewitz would call 'the fog of war'.

Guerrillas in the mist

During the Civil War, James Graham, the Marquess of Montrose, won a series of battles for the Royalists in Scotland. However, in 1645, Montrose and his cavalry had taken up quarters in Selkirk, while his infantry were camped two miles away at Philiphaugh. On 14 September, a Parliamentary army under Sir David Leslie managed to advance on them through the morning fog without being seen. Montrose was alerted by the sound of gunfire. By the time he arrived, it was too late. The camp had been over-run. Turning tail, Montrose managed to escape the slaughter with thirty men. He was unable to raise another army. The Royalist cause lost, he went into exile with Charles II, only to return to Scotland in 1650 with 1,200 men. After another defeat he was hanged in Edinburgh that May, all because of a morning mist.

Cádiz cock-up

In 1588, the English navy under Sir Francis Drake and Sir John Hawkins defeated the Spanish Armada, partly because of a storm at sea. Thirty-seven years later, ambitious courtier George Villiers, the first Duke of Buckingham, decided that he would have another crack at the Spanish. Drake had opened hostilities with an attack on Cádiz. In just thirty-six hours, he had destroyed thousands of tons of supplies and shipping destined for the Armada in an action he called 'singeing the King of Spain's beard'. Buckingham thought he would do the same.

But Buckingham was not an experienced sea dog like Drake, who had circumnavigated the world in 1577–80 and plundered the Spanish Main. A royal favourite and most likely the king's lover, the handsome Buckingham was made Lord High Admiral because of his good looks and used his position to secure lucrative appointments for his family. At the time James I was trying to make an alliance with Spain and sent his son Charles to marry the King of Spain's daughter. Snubbed by the Infanta, he returned home to demand that England declare war on Spain. When he came to the throne, Charles began raising money for the venture. However, the City and international investors had little faith in Buckingham and money remained a problem. Nevertheless, the expedition to Cádiz went ahead in 1625.

Ill-armed armada

Seeking to dispense his patronage, Buckingham appointed relations and friends to senior positions. Of the six commanders, not one had experience of maritime warfare. Under them were a fleet of ninety ships. Many were survivors of the Armada, now rotten hulks and with ragged sails. Others were Newcastle coal ships pressed into service. They were old and slow. This was not the fleet Drake had commanded.

Nor was this going to be a hit-and-run action, a mere 'singeing of the King of Spain's beard'. Eager to outdo Drake, Buckingham planned a full-scale invasion. He assembled an army of ten thousand men. But these were no bristling redcoats. They were a ragtag rabble of pressed men. Wealthy recruits could buy themselves out, so Buckingham was left with jailbirds, beggars, simpletons and the dregs of society. Nor were they imposing physical specimens. When a senior officer inspected 2,500 of them, he reported that two hundred were physically defective. Twenty-six were over sixty. Twenty-four were seriously ill. Four were blind. One was raving mad; another a church minister. Others were maimed, simple-minded or deformed. One man had no feet; another had one leg nine inches shorter than the other. There was a sixty-year-old father of eleven children who had been picked because he had had a row with a local alderman. An elderly man, who was blind, had been sent because he had given evidence against the brother of a constable.

Some of the officers complained that their men had 'nothing to hide their nakedness'. They had no money, either. When the local farmers in Dorset and Devon they had been billeted on found this out, they refused to feed them. Riots ensued. Starving soldiers roamed the countryside, killing sheep to feed themselves. The authorities had to disarm them. Consequently, these raw recruits got no weapons training.

There was relief among the ranks when Buckingham, who had intended to lead the expedition himself, grew sick and was forced to appoint Sir Edward Cecil instead. Cecil had proved his abilities as a soldier in campaigns in the Netherlands. However, he had one major drawback. He knew nothing of the sea.

Ill-provisioned

Despite everything, the fleet set sail from Plymouth on 5 October 1625, returning the next day because of bad weather. It set out again on 8 October. Just a few miles out, the king's ship *Lion* was found to be leaking and had to return to port. After only three days at sea, it was found that the fleet did not have enough provisions and rations had to be cut to a quarter. The food that had been supplied by the foppish quartermaster Sir James Bagg, a Buckingham appointee, was largely mouldy and the water infected. Large numbers of men were poisoned.

They had set out late in the season and gales blew up in the Bay of Biscay. Several ships sank. Cecil's flagship, the *Ann Royal*, was badly damaged when her cannons broke loose and pitched freely across the gun decks. The damage was so extensive that she stayed afloat only with constant pumping.

When the storm blew itself out, Sir Edward Cecil, the only experienced military man on board, called a shipboard council of war to assess the situation. Another ship was leaking so badly, she wanted to return to port. Cecil begged her to stay. Others reported that the gunpowder and food were soaked and the fresh water contaminated. Then it was found that the shot they had bought did not fit the muskets. The moulds for making new shot were warped and the muskets themselves were so badly made that they had no touch-holes.

Not only were they practically unarmed, they had lost half their ships. During the storm the Earl of Essex's squadron had become detached. Things became even more dire as they approached the Spanish coast and sighted what they took to be enemy ships. Fortunately, they sailed away and Cecil detached some of his fastest ships to give chase, thinking that they were treasure ships bringing gold and silver from South America. Cecil may have been a battle-hardened soldier, but he betrayed his lack of knowledge of the sea. The treasure convoys made the crossing earlier in the year and were already safely in port. The ships *his* ships were chasing were some of Essex's missing squadron who had failed to signal.

Reaching Cádiz, Cecil ordered Essex to enter the Puerto de Santa Maria opposite Cádiz and find an anchorage for the fleet where they could take on much-needed fresh water. Instead, Essex sailed into Cádiz and single-handedly attacked the twelve galleons and fifteen galleys that were at anchor there. Only the intervention of the entire fleet saved Essex from destruction. The English had now shown their hand.

Up the creek

Seeing the size of the English fleet – if not its condition – the Spanish ships cut their cables and fled up the narrow creek of Puerto Real. Essex failed to follow them, now claiming that he had no specific orders to engage the Spaniards. Cecil called another council of war. Meanwhile, an English sailor who escaped from the port reported to Cecil that the Spaniards had been caught unawares and Cádiz was protected by only a small garrison. An immediate attack would take the city. With the Spanish galleons trapped in the Puerto Real, where they could be picked off by the English at their leisure, this seemed like a good plan. However, some of Cecil's more cautious officers insisted that he take the fort of Puntales first.

Three English men-of-war began the bombardment, while five ships supplied by England's Dutch ally and twenty conscripted Newcastle collier vessels, which drew less draft, were sent inshore. But the collier captains, unwilling to risk their ships – and their livelihoods – hung back. The Dutch ships were badly shot up; one ran aground. Essex's squadron intervened. Then, when the colliers reluctantly unleashed a few long shots, one of them took off the stern of Essex's flagship. The bombardment ceased. Twenty-four hours later, a small landing party took the fort, only to discover that, though the English fleet had expended two thousand rounds bombarding it, the fort was undamaged.

However, the bombardment had had one effect: it had roused the Spaniards for miles around. Spanish troops were now rushing to the defence of Cádiz. Even though he thought he was still up against a small garrison, Cecil decided to disembark his entire army. When he then heard that more Spaniards were on their way, Cecil led eight thousand men to cut them off at Zuazo Bridge, which connected the port to the mainland. They marched across the salt flats of Leon.

Under a blazing sun and in the salty atmosphere, they built up a terrible thirst. They had brought no food or water with them and one regiment turned back. The rest camped for the night near a deserted building, which turned out to be a wine store. As the men had had nothing to drink or eat, Cecil took pity on them and ordered one barrel of wine to be issued to each regiment. With nothing in their stomachs, the men got wildly drunk. Eager to get drunker, they broke into the wine store. Mayhem ensued. In an attempt to restore order, Cecil commanded that the wine be poured away. The men scooped it up in their helmets and threat-

ened any officer who tried to stop them. They then turned on Cecil, whose bodyguard had to fire into the mob. That night, Cecil wrote, his entire army could have had their throats slit and been routed by just three hundred of the enemy.

Hung over

In the morning, the men were so hung over they had to return to Puntales. Around a hundred were left to sleep

13

it off in ditches, where they were later butchered by the Spaniards. When he returned to the fleet, Cecil discovered that the Spanish had sunk four hulks across the mouth of the creek, preventing a naval attack on the Spanish ships trapped there.

That night it poured with rain and troops spent a dismal night in the open in sodden fields outside Cádiz. Next morning they re-embarked, disheartened, and the fleet sailed out of the harbour – without even taking on fresh water or supplies – to the cheers and jeers of the citizens of Cádiz, who remained, that time, remarkably unsinged.

Plague and penury

On the voyage back to England, plague broke out on the ships. Some ships were so badly hit that no one was well enough to sail them. So Cecil came up with a brilliant plan. Two men from each of the healthy ships would be exchanged with two from the plague-ridden vessels. This had the effect of spreading the plague throughout the entire fleet. A storm then scattered the ships. On 11 December, the *Ann Royal* limped into Kinsale in southern Ireland with six feet of water in the hold. It was manned by 160 sick and 130 dead. Throughout that winter, other ships hobbled home, crewed by the dead and dying.

The survivors were shunned. One commander wrote, 'They stink as they go, the poor rags they have are rotten and ready to fall if they are touched. The soldiers are sick and naked, and the officers are moneyless and friendless, not able to feed themselves.'

Sir John Eliot, formerly a supporter of Buckingham, told Parliament, 'Our honour is ruined, our ships are sunk, our men perished, not by the sword, not by the enemy, not by chance, but . . . by those we trust.'

But it was Cecil, not Buckingham, who shouldered most of the blame. Newly created Viscount Wimbledon, Cecil was lampooned as Viscount Sitstill for failing to take on the enemy. Nevertheless, he was appointed Lord Lieutenant of Surrey and Governor of Portsmouth, and made a Privy Councillor. At sixty-three, he married a seventeen-year-old, gave her a child and died soon after.

Retreat from La Rochelle

While the remnants of the disastrous Cádiz expedition were limping home, the Duke of Buckingham was making more trouble. He sent ships to aid the French, who were besieging the Protestant Huguenots in La Rochelle. When the Huguenot fleet was destroyed, Buckingham, who was suspected of being a Catholic, was blamed.

Parliament sought to impeach Buckingham. To prevent this, the king simply dissolved Parliament. To counter the charges made against him, Buckingham decided to back the Huguenots and break the blockade of La Rochelle by invading the island of Ré, which dominated the approaches. With Parliament dissolved, the king had no access to money.

15

Buckingham promised to pay for everything while relying on the king's ability to raise funds by means of obtaining forced loans from unwilling citizens.

Bottomless Bagg

Shortage of cash meant Buckingham would have to re-use the ships that had limped back from Cádiz, even those that had been veterans of the Armada. Sir James Bagg was called upon, once again, to provide the provisions. When this put him £10,000 in debt, Buckingham authorised Bagg to sell some cargoes of salt. However, he sold the contents of the *Costly* of Dover, which had been earmarked to salt the fleet's victuals. Bagg made a considerable profit on the sale, earning him the nickname 'Bottomless Bagg'.

More troops were levied, but they turned out to be the same quality as before. Inland counties sent 'poor rogues and beggars', who were in poor physical shape and practically naked – 'such creatures as I am ashamed to describe them', one observer of the Hampshire levies said. Buckingham ordered the lords of the shires to 'take more care to send young and able-bodied men, well-clothed and fit for service'. But none of the counties were going to send their best young men to die abroad when, traditionally, foreign expeditions had been a good opportunity to get rid of undesirables. Besides, Buckingham had no money and both his soldiers and crew went unpaid throughout. He even cut back on his personal preparations, spending no more than a few thousand pounds on silk, linen and his own favourite gold and silver buttons.

Looking the part

Despite his lack of military experience, Buckingham did not invite Sir Edward Cecil, who had led the expedition to Cádiz, to join the attack on Ré. Instead he decided to compensate by at least looking the part.

'His serious intention is also shown by the military costume which he wears, with an immense collar and magnificent plume of feathers in his hat,' wrote an observer.

He also took velvet and satin suits as leisurewear for the evenings, along with his personal harpist and £50 worth of books to keep himself entertained during lulls in the battle. While his men would have to survive on Mr Bagg's mouldy and unsalted rations, Buckingham took goats, chickens, oxen and milch cows for his own personal sustenance. He also took a coach and horses with a full retinue of coachmen, pages and footmen. However, his most prized possession was an ornate icon of Louis XIII's with Anne of Austria, the King of Spain's daughter, which he worshipped daily aboard his flagship, which was named – inappropriately, as it turned out – *Triumph*. In all, Buckingham's personal expenditure came to just £10,000 – enough to equip and maintain a regiment for six months.

Seven regiments of a thousand men were assembled. They were led by experienced officers. Unfortunately, the officers had earned their experience at Cádiz. The Earl of Essex, who had done so much to screw up the attack on Cádiz, was offered a regiment but, fortunately, refused. Their send-off from Portsmouth was accompanied by crowds booing from the dockside and chants wishing the fleet such speed as to lose the 'graceless Duke'. In all, there were more than a hundred ships with his, forty supplied by the king. This may have looked impressive, but the warships were outrun by pirates they gave chase to in the Channel.

Unimpressed

The fleet landed off the southeast tip of Ré on 12 July 1627. Buckingham sent his personal secretary, Sir William Becher, to tell the Huguenots in La Rochelle that Buckingham had come to save them, but the Huguenots were enjoying a religious fast at the time and were unimpressed that help was at hand. Nevertheless, Buckingham was determined to go ahead with his plan. The capture of Ré, he was convinced, would be a humiliation to Louis XIII's chief minister, Cardinal Richelieu, who was commanding the siege.

He sent a boy to reconnoitre the situation. He was to swim ashore, then run a mile inland to see whether there were any French soldiers about. There were. They chased him back to the beach, but he managed to make it back to the *Triumph* to report that the coast was unfortified. Unfortunately, the sight of a naked boy running around had alerted the French to the fact that there was an English fleet offshore and, from the top of the mast, Buckingham's lookouts could see formations of French soldiers drawing up. Now he was going to have to fight his way ashore.

After being cooped up in a hold for weeks, all the first men ashore wanted to do was lie in the surf. This left them vulnerable when the French infantry advanced with fifteen-foot pikes. When Buckingham landed, he drove his men up the beach, clearing the French infantry from the sand. In response, the French cavalry galloped in to cut them down.

The carnage continued until about a thousand English had landed. They formed themselves up into a square, protected by pikes, which the French cavalry could not penetrate. Musketeers within the square began shooting the French down. The French infantry returned to the fray but, after finding that their pikes were a good deal shorter than those of the English, they resorted to throwing stones.

Eventually, the French commander Jean Caylar d'Anduze de Saint-Bonnet, Marquis de Toiras, later promoted Marshal of France, withdrew his men to the citadel of St Martin de Ré. Instead of pursuing the retreating troops, Buckingham ordered his men to dig in on the beach, losing the initiative. Had he gone on the offensive, he could have taken the whole island that day.

Buckingham was no modern military man. He looked back to an older era of chivalry. When three injured French nobleman asked to be allowed to go to the mainland to have their wounds dressed, Buckingham sent his barge, which was lined with scarlet fabric, and musicians to soothe their passage.

Sitting it out in the citadel

Although several of Buckingham's leading officers had already been killed, he quickly took possession of the town of St Martin de Ré. But Toiras was secure within the citadel and there was little Buckingham could do about it. The English siege engineer had drowned during the landing and the cannons they had brought were too few and too small. However, Buckingham's master gunner assured him that everything would be okay once he had them set up. As a demonstration, he blasted away at some nearby windmills. Infuriated at this needless destruction, the French opened fire, silencing the English guns in a matter of minutes.

Nevertheless, the French were short of water and provisions, and any attempt to supply them from the mainland was sure to be intercepted by the English fleet. So Buckingham could safely have left them there and gone on to relieve the Huguenots in La Rochelle. But he decided that the demands of chivalry required he take the citadel first, so he committed his men to a long and unnecessary siege.

When they began digging in, the line of trenches were too far from the citadel walls, beyond musket range. For nearly six weeks, the English occupied them in perfect safety. On the other hand, they were unable to inflict any casualties on the garrison. Then, when they began to dig some more trenches nearer to the citadel, an English officer reported that the French 'cheerily told us that they thought we had been lost and wondered where we had lain hidden the while'.

As it was, the second series of trenches were of as little use as the first. The new chief engineer had been a humble labourer before being pressed into service and built the fortification on the wrong side of the ditch. Eventually, Buckingham got his own gardener to design the earthworks.

It was a wet summer to spend in the trenches. The food was poor and disease started to take its toll. Sir William Becher had mustered another four hundred men in Portsmouth, but the transports needed to take them to France were held up in the Thames waiting for the munitions they had ordered to be released by the ordinance department. Buckingham seconded another five hundred men from the fleet, but the siege was still woefully undermanned. Nevertheless, Buckingham was on sure ground as long as he could prevent French supply ships reaching the garrison.

To this end, he asked his engineers, who had already proved their incompetence, to find a way of blockading the harbour entrance. They devised a floating stockade of masts and timbers chained together. This was soon broken up by the waves. Next, they arranged a pontoon with ships lashed together. Buckingham was delighted, boasting that 'not even a bird' could get through to St Martin. A storm broke this up, too, ripping the ships from their anchors. Then they tried a floating island of upturned boats, which English soldiers were supposed to take shelter under and see off the French supply ships. The wind lifted them from the water and the waves smashed them to pieces.

Cash strapped

Buckingham then received news that no more money was going to be forthcoming from the king. Becher raised £10,000 of the £14,000 Buckingham needed to keep his army in the field. Meanwhile, Buckingham grew so desperate that he wrote to his mother, but she had just bought a new house and had problems of her own. His wife sent £200 from the housekeeping, but reminded him that the roof needed fixing.

Despite the shortage of money, the standards of chivalry must not be allowed to slip. While English lived in squalor in the trenches, the Marquis de Toiras sent a polite note asking whether there were any melons on the island. Buckingham sent him a dozen. In return the marquis sent him half a dozen bottles of fragrant orange-flower water and boxes of Cyprus powder, which was used as a cosmetic. Buckingham sent these on to his wife, but she threw them away, fearing they might be poisoned. Buckingham then grew petulant and had the island's Catholic women and children forced into the citadel to put pressure on the garrison's dwindling food supplies.

Some two thousand Irish reinforcements arrived in September. But a Scottish supply fleet carrying five thousand men was broken up by a storm off Norfolk. Nevertheless the arrival of more men convinced the French that the English were not about to leave. Toiras called for three volunteers to swim ashore and tell Richelieu of their plight. Only one made it, but he was able to inform the Cardinal of the garrison's parlous state.

Terms of surrender

Meanwhile, the marquis sent an officer to negotiate the terms of surrender with Buckingham. Ever gallant, Buckingham praised the bravery of the garrison and asked the officer to return the following day. After giving the French twenty-four hours' respite, Buckingham then asked Toiras to draw up his own terms of surrender. Three days later Toiras agreed, but asked for a further day to do so. Buckingham, chivalrously, obliged. That night, a fleet of French rowing boats slipped through the English blockade and reprovisioned the garrison. The next morning, the French taunted the English besiegers, appearing on the walls with turkeys and hams on the ends of their pikes.

As Toiras was not about to be starved out, Buckingham's commanders advised him to withdraw before the winter set in. While the French were assembling a new relief fleet, his men were being decimated by disease. Those who were fit enough to fight were still 'bare-arsed' from dysentery. Nevertheless, Buckingham sent them into battle. In one last desperate thrust, they quickly cleared the outer fortifications, then attacked the walls of the citadel itself. It was only then that the English found out that the ladders they had brought were too short. Those who tried to climb the ladders had heavy objects dropped on their heads, while those who milled around below were easy pickings for the French musketeers.

Buckingham finally ordered the evacuation of the island. Meanwhile, the Marshal of France, Henri de Schomberg, landed with an army of six thousand men and tried to cut the English off from their ships. The English had to make their escape over a causeway to Loix. Buckingham had had the foresight to order his engineers to build a redoubt to protect it. Unfortunately, they had built the redoubt at the wrong end. The causeway was five hundred yards long, just four feet wide, with no handrail. Just as the first men set off down it, the French attacked. Caught in the bottleneck at the end, the English were forced, at pike point, into the marshes, where they drowned. Those who reached Loix began a desperate rearguard action. They managed to force the French back, but were in no hurry to pursue them. Instead, they quickly embarked and sailed for home, meeting a convoy of supplies and reinforcements on their way.

Buckingham returned to Portsmouth with only two thousand of the seven thousand men he had set out with. A ballad circulated with the line, 'These things have lost our honour, men surmise: Thy treachery, neglect and cowardice.' And a poem was written commemorating his fresh failure. It read:

> Thou art returned again with all thy faults,
> Thou great commander of the all-go-naughts,
> And left the isle behind thee? What's the matter?
> Did winter make thy teeth to chatter?

But Buckingham would not give up. The following April, he sent another fleet under his brother-in-law, the Earl of Denbigh, who returned without a fight to Portsmouth, saying he had 'no commission to hazard the king's ships'. Parliament was recalled as the king was again short of money. Once again, it tried to impeach Buckingham. Charles heard its petition, then prorogued Parliament once more.

By then, Buckingham had a new plan – to send in

fireships packed with explosives to blow up the sea wall the French were constructing. This time he used his own money to assemble a fleet at Portsmouth. Meanwhile he was besieged by the hungry and destitute survivors from his previous expeditions. And his astrologer John Lambe, whom he frequently consulted, was denounced as the 'Duke's devil' and hacked to death in the street.

'I am the one'

Buckingham was in Portsmouth, preparing to sail, when he was stabbed to death. The assassin was John Felton, a wounded veteran of Buckingham's Cádiz and Ré adventures. He escaped in the confusion but later presented himself to the crowd and, perhaps expecting to be praised, announced, 'I am the one.'

He was immediately seized and taken to the Tower of London, where he was tortured. On the way, he was being taken through Kingston when an old woman cried out, 'God bless thee, little David', for he was thought to have slain Goliath. Felton was celebrated throughout the country. Stitched inside his hatband were two statements justifying his deeds. He explained that 'the remonstrance of the house of parliament' convinced him that by killing the duke he 'should do his country great service'. He was, he said, prepared to 'make himself a martyr for his country'. Copies of Felton's hatband statements were circulated. Stories of his words and deeds were told in the streets or scrawled into newsletters. Toasts were drunk in Dover alehouses and Oxford butteries. Poems celebrated his actions, hailing him as a patriotic hero, God's agent, England's deliverer. Buckingham was portrayed as cowardly, effeminate and popish, while Felton was manly, brave and Protestant.

Nevertheless, he was tried, convicted and hanged at Tyburn on 29 November 1628. His body was cut down and taken to Portsmouth, where it was hung in chains to rot. Buckingham, of course, was buried in Westminster Abbey, a national hero. His debts were cleared by the crown. Meanwhile 'Bottomless Bagg' died owing some £60,000, even though he had been accused of laying the cost of billeting the survivors of the Ré expedition on the country rather than using money left for this purpose by the duke. By then, Buckingham's fleet had sailed under Robert Bertie, the Earl of Lindsey, who had already failed in a second expedition to seize the South American treasure ships heading for Cádiz. He failed to relieve La Rochelle in September 1628 and the Huguenots surrendered the following month.

Breaking French windows with guineas

In the late seventeenth century, the English continued their old rancour at the French by making 'descents' on French ports along the French coast or in the West Indies. This costly policy of harassment became known as 'breaking French windows with guineas'. It was stopped when William of Orange came to the British throne in 1689. He had experience of fighting the French on the Continent and told the English that their attacks caused France no more damage than if Louis XIV had stubbed his toe.

Victory in the Battle of La Hogue off the coast of

Normandy in 1692 gave England command of the Channel, and the English were determined to prove themselves to their new king, so they planned an amphibious assault on Brest. The operation was not to be under the command of an experienced Dutch or German general, but an Englishman – Thomas Talmash, a rival of the famed John Churchill, Earl, later Duke, of Marlborough.

Marlborough promptly wrote to the exiled James II, whom he had helped depose, telling him of Talmash's expedition. James was a guest of Louis XIV at the time. Louis rushed an additional four thousand troops to the area and sent the famous military engineer Sébastien Vauban, who installed an extra three hundred cannons and ninety mortars. Meanwhile, the Royal Navy attacked a French convoy in Camaret Bay, just outside the entrance to Brest harbour. Vauban immediately assumed that they were spying out beaches for a landing, and increased the defences there too.

Not only did the French know that the English were coming, the English *knew* they knew. London newspapers carried a daily 'Letter from Brest'. On 4 June, it reported that four hundred cannons surrounded the port and the strength of the garrison had reached nine thousand. Nevertheless, Talmash set off from England with six thousand men, arriving in Camaret Bay on 7 June 1694. Almost immediately a huge mortar hit an English man-of-war two and a half miles out to sea. The bomb went straight through the deck and the keel. It was plain that the English ships would not be able to give any landing force covering fire.

That afternoon, Talmash went ashore and, apparently, found no sign of any Frenchmen or entrenchments. However, on board ship, the admiral, Lord Carmarthen, recorded that the French were found to be 'much better prepared on all sides, with mortars, guns and men, than we expected'.

The following morning, Carmarthen began his bombardment as ordered. This, of course, proved ineffective. Once the smoke cleared, a flotilla of small boats under Lord Cutts set out. On shore, the French could hardly believe their eyes. The bay was full off undefended boats filled with English soldiers who could be picked off by cannon, chain-shot and musket fire, almost at will. Seeing the assault stall, Talmash jumped into a rowing boat. Nearing Cutts, he shouted out, 'My lord, is this following of orders? Do you see how the boats are in disorder? Pray, my lord, let us land in as good order as we can.'

By then the fleet was also under attack, but Talmash would not be halted. In his *History of England*, Thomas Babington Macaulay wrote,

Batteries which had then escaped notice opened on the ships a fire so murderous that several decks were soon cleared. Great bodies of foot and horse were discernible; and, by their uniforms, they appeared to be regular troops. The young Rear Admiral [Carmarthen] sent an officer in all haste to warn Talmash. But Talmash was so completely possessed by the notion that the French were not prepared to repel an attack that he disregarded all cautions and would not even trust his own eyes. He felt sure that the force which he saw assembled on the shore was a mere rabble of peasants, who had been brought together in haste from the surrounding country.

Confident that these mock soldiers would run like sheep before real soldiers, he ordered his men to pull for the beach. He was soon undeceived.

Determined to set an example, Talmash landed with one officer and nine grenadiers. The beach he thought was undefended was just three hundred yards long. It was defended by three trenches, each manned by 150 French musketeers. Talmash rushed forward and took cover behind some rocks. A further two hundred grenadiers landed and Talmash led them in a charge on the French positions. They were cut down almost to a man, leaving Talmash standing virtually alone. The French cavalry then charged down the beach. The remaining grenadiers threw down their weapons and surrendered. Talmash had to be dragged back to the sea. His boat had been abandoned by its crew and Lord Berkeley offered some sailors £5 to go and rescue him. Meanwhile, other retreating troops found their boat stranded high and dry by the retreating tide. According to the English, three hundred soldiers had been lost in the raid. But a French account says,

> ... on the English side, 800 of the troops from the landing force were killed or wounded, 400 men killed on the ships of the line, and 466 taken prisoner, including 16 officers. The French, according to reports prepared the same day by Monsieur de Langeron and Monsieur de Saint-Pierre, only had around 45 wounded, including 3 officers, including the engineer Traverse, who lost an arm.

29

Back on the *Dreadnought*, Talmash held one final council of war, which decided that the fleet should return to England. He reached Plymouth on 11 June, where he was

seen by surgeons. The prognosis was good, but the following afternoon his leg swelled up and he died. Unable to defend himself, Talmash became the perfect scapegoat, while Marlborough went on to become England's greatest general.

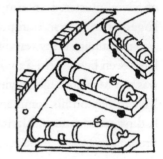

Making a mess at Malplaquet

At the beginning of the eighteenth century, the European powers fell out over who should wear the crown of Spain. Louis XIV of France put his grandson, a Bourbon, on the throne, while others thought the throne belonged to a Habsburg. After seven years of war, in which the French were repeatedly thrashed by allied troops under the Duke of Marlborough and Prince Eugène of Savoy, Louise XIV conceded the Spanish throne to the Habsburgs. However, when the British insisted that the French king use his own troops to remove his grandson, he refused, and the war resumed. There followed the Battle of Malplaquet in September 1709.

For Marlborough there was no point in fighting the battle. The French had already conceded the Spanish throne and they would not be any worse off strategically if they lost – indeed, they would have a smaller army to remove

Louis's grandson from the Spanish throne. But a French victory – or even a draw – would restore France's standing as a military power. Nevertheless, Marlborough and Eugène of Savoy mustered an army of a hundred thousand – the largest army seen in Europe to date – to face the French.

Such a huge army was difficult to manoeuvre and might have been better suited to defence rather than attack. That was not Marlborough's style. But to attack meant he would have to rely on his commanders in the field. As the Dutch had provided troops, Marlborough could hardly refuse the Prince of Orange a role and put him in command of the left wing.

The attack was going to begin with an artillery bombardment, then an advance of the right under Reichsgraf Marshal Johann Matthias von der Schulenburg. After half an hour, the Prince of Orange was supposed to slowly advance the left as a diversionary tactic. Instead, his thirty squadrons of horses charged the French line, unaware that Marshal Boufers had put twenty cannons in a wood to the flank. Canister and grapeshot from the front and side cut the charging cavalry to pieces. Within thirty minutes, they had suffered five thousand casualties and the Prince of Orange had had two horses shot from underneath him. But they continued to attack the cannons. They were followed by the infantry, who were cut to pieces. The famous Dutch Blue Guards were practically annihilated. In a second attack the generals Hamilton and Spaar were lost.

On the right Schulenberg had progressed more slowly. Eventually, he broke through the French defence, but at great cost. Then Marlborough received a message telling

31

him of the situation on the left wing. He and Eugène of Savoy arrived there in time to stop the Prince of Orange making a third attack. Nevertheless, the allies pressed home their advantage. Marlborough broke through in the centre and the French were forced to quit the field. By then Marlborough had lost 24,000 men, against the French 12,000. Still, he considered the battle a victory.

But the huge casualty figures led the Whigs to be driven from office by a Tory landslide at the next election. They committed Britain to being a sea power, rather than fighting on land. Marlborough was dismissed and went into exile, accused of misappropriating public funds. He was returned to favour after George I came to the throne in 1714, but lived in retirement until his death in 1722.

Wild Geese droppings

During the War of the Spanish Succession, Marlborough also found himself up against a brigade of Irishmen fighting for Louis XIV, who were bolstered by British deserters and ex-prisoners of war. These were the Wild Geese. The French Irish Brigade was originally formed from the remnants of the Jacobite army that had lost to William of Orange at the Battle of the Boyne in 1691 and surrendered at Limerick the following year. But the victorious William let them leave for France. They fought against William in the Nine Years' War, but were disbanded in 1698 under the Treaty of Ryswick. But Louis called on the fighting Irish again in 1700 and, two years later, they won an unexpected victory against Marlborough's sidekick, Prince Eugène of Savoy.

An allied army under Prince Eugène attacked the French at Chiari on 1 September 1701, driving them from the field. Louis's army fell back on the town of Cremona, where on 1 February 1702 they were caught in a night attack. The French garrison, under Marshal François de Neufville, Duc de Villeroi, was taken completely by surprise. A small unit under Prince Eugène himself launched a commando-style attack, which succeeded in capturing the Duc de Villeroi and other high-ranking French officers. A thousand French soldiers were killed in the attack, many of them in their sleep. But the assault was not a complete success. A large allied force under Charles Thomas de Lorraine-Vaudemont was to have taken the Po gate into Cremona, but this was held by the Irish Brigade.

Just twenty-five men under Captain Stuart held off the Austrians until reinforcements under Major Daniel O'Mahony reached them. As the Austrian losses mounted, Prince Eugène sent one of his own Wild Geese, Francis MacDonnell, to bribe them. 'Countrymen,' he said, 'Prince Eugène sends me to say to you, that if you will change [sides], you shall have higher pay in the Imperial army than you have had in the French service . . . If you reject [this offer], I do not see how you can escape certain destruction. We are masters of the city, with the exception of your post. It is on this account, his Highness only awaits my return to attack you with the greatest part of his force, and to cut you to pieces, should you not accept his offers.'

O'Mahony replied, 'Prince Eugène seems to fear us more than he esteems us, since he causes such propositions to be made to us. We wish to gain the esteem of the Prince by doing our duty, not by cowardice or treachery, unworthy of men of honour.' The indignant O'Mahony then made MacDonnell his prisoner.

When Prince Eugène realised that MacDonnell was not coming back, he asked the captured Duc de Villeroi to order the Irish to surrender or he would be forced to put them all to the sword. De Villeroi said he had 'no longer any orders to give in the town'. The Austrians then attacked in force and were slaughtered. The Irish held out until 3 p.m., when they were finally ordered back. On the way, they blew up the bridge, stranding the main Austrian force on the wrong side of the river. Prince Eugène then found that the other gates to the city were also held by Irishmen. Eventually, Prince Eugène began to see that the city was becoming a trap, rather than a prize, and left without taking the citadel. It was said that Cremona was 'taken by a miracle, and lost by a greater one'.

The Wild Geese gave the English another bloody nose at the Battle of Fontenoy in May 1745. Their attack against the British right forced the British to withdraw with 50 per cent losses. 'Cursed be the laws which deprived me of such subjects,' said King George II. Fontenoy was a famous defeat for the English commander, the Duke of Cumberland, George II's son, who went on to brutally suppress the Jacobite Rising at the Battle of Culloden in April 1746 – his only military victory.

With the failure of the Rising, all the hope of a Stuart returning to the British throne was gone. But a trickle of young Irishmen still fled their homeland to join the Irish Brigade, along with British deserters. The majority of the recruits came from the counties of Clare, Limerick, Cork, Kerry and Galway. When they were taken to France by the French ships that arrived on the west coast smuggling in brandy and wine, captains would list the departing Irishmen on their manifests as 'Wild Geese'.

During the Seven Years' War (1756–63), the French fielded six regiments of Irish foot, plus one cavalry unit. As time passed, these units became increasingly less Irish in composition. By the end of the eighteenth century even the officers came from families who had been in France for several generations and were French in all but name.

With the outbreak of the French Revolution the Irish Brigade ceased to exist. It was disbanded on 21 July 1791. Many considered that their oath had been sworn to Louis XVI, who was deposed, and left the service. The rest were absorbed into the infantry of the line. However, after the failure of the Irish Rebellion of 1798, Napoleon Bonaparte raised a small Irish unit from the exiled veterans.

Other Wild Geese fought in the armies of Austria, Poland, Russia, Spain and Sweden. They also fought in South America and with the French Army of General Rochambeau, who helped defeat the British at Yorktown.

CHAPTER TWO

Ludicrous Leaders

ATTLES TURN PARTICULARLY BEASTLY – and bloodthirsty – when mad, bad or just plain incompetent men are in charge. There is a wry irony that useless generals who squander their own men's lives are almost invariably rewarded with promotions, titles, honours, plaudits and statues in public places.

Drawing fire

On 13 September 1758, during the French and Indian War in North America, Major James Grant led more than eight hundred men to reconnoitre the French-held Fort Duquesne, the site of modern Pittsburgh, ahead of the main British column. Arriving two miles from the fort, Grant sent fifty men forward to scout. They set fire to a storehouse and returned.

In case this was not enough to warn the French of their presence, Grant marched his men up to the fort the following morning accompanied by pipes and drums. As he was not supposed to take the fort, just reconnoitre it, men were sent forward to sketch the French defences. They were sitting in front of the fort sketching away when the gates opened and a large force of French and Indians came out. They killed some 342 of Grant's men, taking others – including Grant – prisoner.

When the main Anglo-American force arrived, the French had burnt the fort and abandoned it. With the Virginian contingent with the Royal American Regiment was a loyal subject of the British crown named George Washington. Four years earlier, he had led a surprise attack on a detachment of thirty Frenchmen, killing the commander, Coulon de Jumonville, and nine others, taking the rest prisoner. This precipitated the French and Indian War, which ended in 1763 after the British had driven the French out of the Ohio River valley. An attempt to tax the American colonists to pay for the war led to the American Revolution, as the colonists no longer needed protection from the French and their Indian allies.

After the French and Indian War, Grant became governor of Florida, then an MP. In a speech in the run-up

to the War of Independence, he said that the colonists could not fight and he could 'get from one end of America to the other and geld all the males'. When he found he could not live up to that boast, he proposed burning Boston, New York and Philadelphia. At the Battle of Long Island in 1776, he let most of the colonial force escape. He also proved less than effective against Marquis de Lafayette and was dispatched to the West Indies. Nevertheless he was made a full general in 1796 and became Laird of Ballindalloch.

Unfit to serve

In October 1758, the Duke of Marlborough died unexpectedly, leaving Lord George Sackville, who had been with him at St Malo, in command in Germany. At Minden, the Allies scored an unexpected victory against the French, and Prince Ferdinand of Brunswick, who was commanding the Allied force, ordered Sackville to send his cavalry to pursue the fleeing French to complete their destruction. Instead, he advanced slowly and not in the direction instructed. The order was repeated several times. Each time Sackville did nothing. When his deputy, the Marquis of Granby, moved up, Sackville ordered him back – it is thought to deny him any glory. Ferdinand was so exasperated that he wrote to George II, saying that, if Granby had commanded the cavalry, his victory over the French would have been complete.

Soon after, pamphlets flooded London accusing Sackville of everything from cowardice to sodomy. In an attempt to redeem his good name, Sackville demanded a court martial. But rather than being exonerated, he was cashiered and was judged to be unfit to serve the king in any military capacity whatsoever. The king personally struck Sackville's name from the list of privy councillors and had the fact reported in the *London Gazette*. The sentence was published in army orders and read out on parade grounds – an unprecedented act. It was said that these were 'censures much worse than death to a man who has any sense of honour'.

But all was not lost for Sackville. When George II died in 1760, he resumed his place in the House of Commons. Then, as Lord Germain, he joined the government of Lord North and served as Secretary of State for America during the War of Independence, adding another failure to his far-from-distinguished career.

Rallying call

In the winter of 1776, George Washington needed a victory. After a series of defeats, he had abandoned New York and withdrawn to Pennsylvania to defend Philadelphia, the rebels' capital. The British commander, Sir William Howe, assumed that the fighting season was over and moved his troops into winter quarters. It was then that Washington came up with the daring plan to cross the Delaware River and attack the British at Trenton, New Jersey. He got lucky. In command of the German mercenaries from Hess holding Trenton was Colonel Johann Gottlieb Rall.

Rall was a professional soldier who had fought in the War of Austrian Succession, the Jacobite Rebellion, the Seven Years' War and the Fourth Russo-Turkish War. He had little time for a ragtag bunch of colonial rebels. He had little time for his own men, either, keeping them on parade in the snow while he wallowed in a warm bath.

When he was advised to fortify the city, he rejected the plan as a sign of weakness. The only defence required against the American rebels was a sharp bayonet, he maintained. Ever vigilant, he spent late nights drinking and playing cards, and slept in late in the mornings. On Christmas Day, Rall received a letter from an American loyalist warning him of Washington's intentions. Nevertheless, the dawn patrol was stood down because of the bitter cold. The remaining pickets kept their backs to the river due to the biting wind, while the rest of the garrison were sleeping off the excesses of Christmas. Consequently, Washington's attack on the morning of 26 December achieved complete surprise.

Hearing shots, an officer went to rouse Rall, who refused to be hurried from his bed. Meanwhile, the men who had been roused were being raked by American grapeshot. When Rall did get up, he summoned a band – a European veteran, he would not think of going into battle without the sound of bugle, fife and drum.

He formed up his men and marched them, half dressed, towards the enemy, who shot them down. The Hessians scattered. In an attempt to rally them, Rall mounted his horse and unsheathed his sword. Thus presenting a better target, he was shot down.

Nearly a thousand Hessians surrendered, along with six guns and the regimental colours. The Americans lost just two men, but not in battle. They froze to death crossing the Delaware.

Unreliable allies

During the Peninsular War (1807–14), Arthur Wellesley, later the Duke of Wellington, found himself allied to a Spanish army under Gregorio García de la Cuesta, a general famed for the fact that he never won a battle. Indeed, Cuesta had suffered a series of defeats at the hands of the French and been trampled by his own cavalry before joining forces with the British.

Like Napoleon, Cuesta had a general disdain for Wellesley as a 'sepoy general' – Wellington's early victories had all been in India. Wellesley had little time for Cuesta, either, considering him old, obstinate and incompetent. As the French approached the River Alberche, where the battle was to take place, Cuesta was nowhere to be seen. When Wellington rode over to the Spanish camp, he found Cuesta asleep. Incoherent when roused, Cuesta promised to fight the next day.

Ignoring Wellesley's assessment of the situation, the following morning Cuesta went off in pursuit of the French, only to find that they had now been reinforced. Hopelessly outnumbered, Cuesta hightailed it back to the River Tagus, where Wellesley had established defensive positions three miles behind the river. But Cuesta refused to cross the river, leaving himself in no-man's-land. If the French attacked, the Spanish would be forced to fight with their backs to the river. Wellesley had to go down on his knees before Cuesta would take up positions behind the river at Talavera.

The Battle of Talavera began when French skirmishers loosed off a few shots. The Spaniards replied with a massive volley. Impressed by their firepower, Wellesley turned to his liaison officer and said, 'If they will but fire as well tomorrow, the day is our own; but as there seems nobody to fire at just now, I wish you would stop it.'

Indeed, they did stop it. The sound and smoke of their own guns sent the Spanish into a panic. They fled the field, shouting 'Treason!' and knocking over the coach the injured Cuesta was travelling in. They then looted the British camp and made off for Portugal, abandoning the wounded British troops left in their care.

As a result, the Battle of Talavera proved bloody but inconclusive, with many of the wounded burnt to death when the grass on the battlefield caught fired. Nevertheless, for this narrow victory, Wellesley was ennobled as 'Viscount Wellington of Talavera and of Wellington'.

'Black Jack' Slade

Not that Wellington's own officers were much better. Sir John 'Black Jack' Slade commanded a hussar brigade at Corunna in October 1808, where he was dismissed as 'nearly useless' and a 'damned stupid fellow'. According to Lord Paget, when Slade was ordered to charge, he kept stopping to adjust his stirrup leathers. At Sahagún that December, Slade gave such a long and stirring speech to his men that they missed the battle.

On another occasion, Sir John Moore noticed Slade carrying a note to the rear during an engagement, a task usually left to a junior aide. Later, Slade brought Moore a report he said his junior officer Colonel Grant had asked him to deliver and Moore enquired whether the major-general had become Colonel Grant's aide-de-camp.

Nevertheless, Slade rose to command the British cavalry in Spain. At Estremadura in 1812, he lost the British their initial advantage by leading a charge down a narrow gorge, only to find the French reserves drawn up at the end – whereupon the brigade panicked and turned tail, losing more than a hundred who were taken prisoner.

It was said that, as cavalry commander, 'He now let no opportunity for inaction pass him – pretending not to comprehend orders which the events passing before him would have made comprehensible to a trumpeter – complaining that his hands were tied, and letting the opportunity slip.'

Naturally, he was awarded a gold medal with cluster, promoted to general and made a baronet.

Military madness

When Sir William Erskine was sent to the Peninsular War, Wellington wrote to the Secretary of War, complaining that he was insane. He had been already confined to a lunatic asylum twice.

'No doubt he is sometimes a little mad,' replied the Secretary, 'but in his lucid intervals he is an uncommonly clever fellow; and I trust he will have no fit during the campaign, though he looked a little wild as he embarked.'

Erskine's eyesight was so bad that he had to be pointed towards the enemy, but Wellington could not dismiss him because of his political influence. He was put in command of the Light Division. In March 1811, Erskine advanced down the main road at Casal Novo in the fog with no scouts. When the fog lifted, he found himself facing a French division deployed for battle with artillery at the ready. It cost the Light Division 155 men.

At the Battle of Sabugal the following month, Erskine again got lost in the fog, allowing the French to escape from the trap Wellington had laid. Then, at the Siege of Almeida, Wellington sent orders telling Erskine to guard a bridge to prevent the small French force escaping. The messenger arrived at four o'clock in the afternoon, when Erskine was still at lunch. Initially, he sent a corporal and four men, but one of his luncheon companions said, 'Sir William, you might as well attempt to block up the bridge with a pinch of snuff.'

Reconsidering, Erskine decided to send a regiment, wrote the orders, but put them in his pocket and forgot about them. When he found them again at about midnight, he finally issued them. A regiment galloped towards the bridge, but it was too late. The French garrison had already escaped.

'They had about 13,000 to watch 1,400,' wrote Wellington. 'There they were all sleeping in their spurs even; but the French got off. I begin to be of the opinion that there is nothing on earth so stupid as a gallant officer.'

Nevertheless, Wellington was forced to praise Erskine in dispatches, though he tried to confine him to positions were he could do the least damage. Eventually, Erskine was declared insane once more and cashiered. In 1813, he committed suicide by jumping out of a window in Lisbon. The attempt was not immediately successful. Lying on the ground dying, he was heard to say, 'Why on earth did I do that?'

Wacky at Waterloo

At Waterloo, the Duke of Wellington was saved by the last-minute arrival of the Prussians under the seventy-two-year-old Prussian Field Marshal Gebhard von Blücher. But Blücher was as mad as a barrel of monkeys. He told Wellington that he had been made pregnant – with an elephant – by a French grenadier. He also claimed that the French heated the floor in his room and he had to dance about on tiptoe.

When the Prussians arrived at Waterloo, where the battle was already raging, their artillery opened fire on the British positions. The British artillery returned fire. When Prussian liaison officers rode over to ask them to stop, they said they would when the Prussians did.

Pickled and preserved

Shortly before his death in 1814, General Robert Rollo Gillespie told his men, 'Every soldier actuated by the principle of cool and deliberate valour will always have the advantage over wild and precipitate courage.' He would have done well to heed these words himself.

At the age of twenty-two, he was a second in a duel. When both men had fired twice and missed, Gillespie suggested that it should be an end to the matter. He then quarrelled with one of the participants and, in a second duel, shot the man dead. A jury of half-pay, reserve officers returned a verdict of justifiable homicide. Later, Gillespie escaped in a rowing boat from a ship adrift on a storm-tossed sea. At Port-au-Prince he braved gunfire to swim ashore carrying a flag of truce. When eight men broke into his house at San Domingo, he killed six of them with a sword; the other two wisely fled. Then he travelled overland to India, where he killed a tiger on the racecourse at Bangalore. Arriving at the fort in Vellore, he found that the sepoys had massacred the Europeans and the 69th Foot were out of ammunition and making their last stand. He had himself hauled into the fort at the end of a rope and rallied the troops. With a detachment of dragoons, he blew the doors off and cut down more than eight hundred of the mutineers.

In Java, though wounded, suffering from fever and faint from exhaustion, he cut a horse from a gun carriage and led a charge that took six thousand prisoners, including two generals. Then, with just fifteen hundred men, he went on to take the fort at Jogjakarta, though it was defended by a hundred guns and thirty thousand men.

At the outbreak of the Anglo-Nepalese War in 1814, Gillespie was sent with a division of Bengali troops to take the fort of Kalanga. For a man of Gillespie's abilities, this should have proved no problem. The fort was garrisoned by no more than 250 Nepalese troops, although they were proving exceedingly stubborn. Gillespie arrived with 4,400 soldiers and decided to attack all four sides of the fort at once. However, three of the columns had to make long detours to get into position to make the attack. A signal – a cannon shot – was to be fired at 10 a.m., warning them to be ready for an assault at midday.

At dawn, Gillespie ordered an artillery bombardment to soften up the defences. This had little effect, other than making Gillespie angry at its ineffectiveness. Rashly, he brought forward the attack to eight o'clock. Over the objections of his officers, he ordered the signal shot be fired. But the other columns took no notice. They were not expecting the signal at that time and another shot could just be part of the softening up.

Three companies of the 53rd Regiment had arrived the previous evening after a long march over arduous terrain. Gillespie had ordered them to rest. Now he countermanded that and ordered them to prepare for action. This caused confusion, especially as the officer who was supposed to command them had left camp. The troops were tired, heavily laden and made slow progress. The impatient Gillespie could not wait for them, so sent in sixty dismounted dragoons – who were promptly hacked to pieces. Then when the men of the 53rd eventually appeared, he cursed them for their tardiness.

At the northwest corner of the fort, there was a small gate. Gillespie ordered cannons to be brought up, but the Nepalese fired first – with grapeshot. Then they ran out of the fort and disabled the undefended guns. Gillespie then berated the 53rd for cowardice, drew his sword and charged the fort single-handed. He was shot dead. At this very moment the support columns burst from the jungle, surrounding the fort, just at the main force were retreating.

Gillespie's successor, Colonel Sebright Mawby, was a more cautious man. He cut off the fort's water supply. After twenty-nine days, the Nepalese came out and ran towards the nearby stream, telling the British they could have the fort they had deserted. However, they did not formally surrender and made off into the jungle.

The men of the 53rd assumed that Gillespie had been drunk during the attack on the fort and were greatly amused when he was put in a barrel of spirits for the trip back to Meerut where he was buried. They said he was 'pickled when alive and preserved when dead'. However, the military historian Sir John Fortescue said that Gillespie was 'the bravest man that ever wore a red coat'. He was commemorated by a sculpture in St Paul's Cathedral and a cenotaph in Calcutta Cathedral.

Onward Christian soldiers

At the Battle of Chillianwala during the Second Sikh War in 1849, the cavalry commander, Brigadier Pope, was such an invalid that he had to be lifted into the saddle. At the sight of the Sikh cavalry, Pope ordered a charge. Or, rather, he meant to. But instead of giving the order 'Threes right!' he said 'Threes about!' At the command, the British horses wheeled around and galloped off the battlefield, knocking over guns and wagons as they went.

The man who prevented a complete rout was the regimental chaplain, a man named Whiting. He leapt out and halted the fleeing troops.

'Halt, sir, or as a minister of the word of God, I'll shoot you,' he said, explaining that God would not allow a Christian army to be hacked to pieces by a pagan horde.

The cavalry rallied and the day was saved, though both sides claimed victory. On the recommendation of the commanding officer, Sir Hugh Gough, Whiting was made bishop.

Leading from the front

During the Crimean War, the British commander, Lord Raglan, achieved something unique in the annals of military history when he single-handedly captured the centre of the Russian position. At sixty-seven, Raglan was rather absent-minded. Recalling his days as secretary to Wellington during the Napoleonic wars, he kept referring to the enemy as the French, who were, in fact, allies at the time. Having ordered four British divisions into a battle, Raglan trotted through a line of French skirmishers in the midst of battle up to the top of Telegraph Hill. Thinking this a good place to site guns, he ordered two cannons to be brought up, which he and his officers used to blow up a Russian ammunition wagon. Convinced they had been outflanked, the Russians withdrew.

Later, Raglan snatched defeat from the jaws of victory at the Battle of Balaclava. Observing the battle from the heights above Sevastopol, Raglan wanted to press home the advantage given by the charge of the Heavy Brigade and take back the heights occupied by the Russians. He sent a note to Lord Lucan, commanding the Light Brigade. It said, 'Cavalry to advance and take advantage of the opportunity to recover the heights. They will be supported by the infantry, which have been ordered to advance on two fronts.'

But Lucan was confused. Where were the infantry? Was he supposed wait for them? For forty-five minutes he did nothing. From the heights, Raglan was infuriated to see the Russians carrying off captured guns. He dictated another note to General Airy, who gave it to his ADC Captain Nolan. It read, 'Lord Raglan wishes the cavalry to advance rapidly to the front – follow the enemy and try to prevent the enemy carrying away the guns . . .'

As Nolan took off, he heard Raglan bark, 'Tell Lord Lucan the cavalry is to attack immediately.'

Again, Lucan was confused. What was he supposed to attack? And, since he was not on heights like Raglan, he could not seen the guns Raglan was referring to. The hotheaded Captain Nolan gestured wildly and shouted, 'There is your enemy! There are your guns!'

The only guns Lucan could see were the Russian artillery at the other end of the valley. It did not occur to him to send someone up to higher ground and assess the situation. Attacking the Russian guns would be suicidal. But Lucan was a soldier. He ordered his brother-in-law Lord Cardigan to lead the Light Brigade in the attack. The two men disliked each other. On several occasions they had come close to exchanging blows in front of the men.

Despite his misgivings, Cardigan had no choice but to obey orders. At the head of 673 men he charged down the valley, only to be overtaken by Captain Nolan, who, to Cardigan's annoyance, had decided to join the attack. He was the first to die. Famously, the French observer General Bosquet, seeing the charge, said, '*C'est magnifique mais ce n'est pas la guerre*' ('It is magnificent, but it is not war'), adding, '*C'est de la folie*' ('It's madness'). A hundred and fifty-six died and 122 were wounded. Many were taken prisoner and 335 horses were killed.

Raglan died of dysentery in the Crimea. He and Captain Nolan, who was also dead and could not defend himself, were blamed for the charge of the Light Brigade. But Cardigan returned to England a hero. He was promoted to inspector general of the cavalry. He even sued an author who claimed he had not led the disastrous charge. Ironically, Cardigan died after falling from a horse in Deene Park, his Northamptonshire seat.

Lord Lucan also prospered. He was made a member of the Order of Bath and promoted general and, ultimately, field marshal.

The redoubtable Redan

During the Siege of Sevastopol during the Crimean War, there were several attacks on two redoubts – with the French assaulting the Malakov and the British the Redan. On 17 June 1855, the French had to change the start time of their assault due to a falling-out between two commanders, but failed to inform Lord Raglan. The signal for the attack was to be a rocket. But, fifteen minutes before the start time, a shell giving off sparks was seen the sky. The French columns were not ready but, mistaking this for the signal rocket, gamely set off. Unfortunately, the Russian gunners were ready and no Frenchmen reached the Malakov alive.

Seeing the French being massacred, Raglan thought, in the cause of Anglo-French unity, the British should be massacred. Four hundred died in the name of the alliance. As they fell back from the Redan, Lieutenant Fisher of the Royal Engineers had left his siege tools at the wall. He stopped Colonel Yea and asked him to fetch them. But as they were talking Yea fell dead with a bullet through his heart. Fisher then asked Captain Jesse, who died with a bullet through the head. Two more officers he asked were decapitated. But, before he could ask a fifth officer, he understandably turned tail and ran.

The French, naturally, blamed the British for the failure of the attack.

The sleeping strategy

Lord Raglan was greatly affected by the failure of the attack on the Redan.

'I hope you are not hurt,' he said to one wounded officer on a stretcher.

Obviously in agony, the man spat at him, told him to go to hell and blamed him for the futile slaughter. Three weeks later Raglan died. Even Florence Nightingale wrote, 'He was not a very great general, but he was a very good man.' She also said it was 'impossible not to love him', but he was hardly the man you wanted as commander-in-chief. But, then again, his replacement was, almost inevitably, a good deal worse.

Sixty-three-year-old General James Simpson had spent most of his military career retired on half-pay. The only thing to recommend him was that he was the tallest man in the army. At a planning meeting for the next assault on Sevastopol in September, General Simpson fell asleep while the strategy was being outlined by the French commander Marshal Aimable Pélissier, who took Simpson's nodding head as a sign of assent. Afterwards, Simpson learnt that the British were to attack the Redan again and they were to begin their assault when they saw the French tricolour flying over the Malakov, which had been pounded by French and British siege guns.

This time the French took the Malakov. The tricolour flying on the top of its tower took Simpson by surprise. He delayed, then he sent a message to General Patrice de Mac-Mahon, who had led the French assault, asking whether he wanted the British to attack the Redan now. Mac-Mahon said he would be very much obliged. Simpson still held back, but then heard from his officers that some hot-headed British troops had gone ahead without even waiting for their siege ladders. They were cut down by the Russian guns, but some reached the wall with bayonets fixed.

A second wave was made up of raw recruits new to Crimea who refused to charge across open ground under gunfire without artillery support and had to be beaten by their officers with the flats of their sabres. Three thousand men were funnelled into an area of less than 2,500 square yards. They were packed so dense that the Russians began dropping heavy stones on their heads. Eventually, they broke, leaving their officers to be shot down. Casualties were 385 killed, 1,886 wounded and 176 missing.

It had all been a complete waste of time – and lives. With the Malakov taken, the Russians abandoned Sevastopol. When British soldiers finally entered the Redan, they found the body of Ensign James Swift of the 90th Foot, the only man to reach the parapet.

Walpole's folly

In 1858, towards the end of the Indian Mutiny – or the First War of Indian Independence as it is now called – Brigadier Walpole was ordered to retake the Rohilkhand region with a column of five to six thousand foot and horse, supported by field and siege guns, and mortars. As they were nearing the fort at Ruiya some fifty miles from Lucknow, they met a British soldier who had just escaped from the fort. He told Walpole that the fort was held by Nirpat Singh. However, Singh was happy to give up the fort, after he had made some token show of resistance.

Consequently, without even scouting the fort, Walpole marched his men up to the imposing front wall. The other three walls were shrouded by jungle and the back wall was so low a child could have climbed over it. Nirpat Singh was, indeed, ready to surrender, but, seeing an entire British column spread out beneath his guns, he found it hard to resist. The defenders opened up, killing more than a hundred British troops. Over half of the Punjab regiment and the 42nd Highlanders were listed as casualties. By the time Walpole had brought up the artillery, Nirpat Singh had evacuated the fort, leaving Walpole to explain his incompetence in dispatches.

Caught napping

'They are incapable of any united military action, and they are moral cowards, so anything they may do will be but a spark in the pan.' This was the assessment of the Boers given by Colonel Sir William Owen Lanyon, administrator of the Transvaal after the British annexed it in 1877. Events soon proved him wrong. On 20 December 1880, a column of 264 soldiers from the 94th Regiment were stopped by a Boer commando at Bronker's Spruit, about thirty-eight miles from Pretoria. Even though the column was surrounded by a thousand Boers dug in on high ground, the English commander Colonel Anstruther refused to turn back. The Boers responded with a hail of bullets. In all, fifty-six were killed and 101 wounded. One man was hit eighteen times and every officer was hit at least once. Anstruther himself died shortly afterwards.

The following month, the British sent a force of a thousand men from Natal. They were commanded by General Sir George Pomeroy Colley. A gifted soldier, he had passed out of the Staff College at Camberley in just ten months – instead of the normal two years – with the highest marks ever recorded. However, he had never exercised independent command in the field and he faced an enemy who outnumbered his force by two to one and knew the terrain well.

Meeting a force of two thousand Boers at Laing's Nek, Colley made a frontal assault. It was the last time the regimental colours were carried into action. He was repulsed with 197 casualties. A second attempt resulted in a further 150 casualties. Colley then decided to take Majuba Hill, which overlooked the Boer positions. A quick victory was essential. William Gladstone had just won the 1880 election and had begun negotiations with the Boers. Colley was eager to seize glory before the war ended. He was urged on by his wife, who was the daughter of Major-General Henry Meade 'Tiger' Hamilton and sister to a future general, Bruce Hamilton.

Colley and 365 men scaled the 6,000-foot peak. From there, they overlooked the Boer camp around a mile and a half away. But, instead of digging in, his troops began waving and jeering at the Boers below. Expecting the Boers to pack up and move on, Colley took a little nap.

But the Boers were made of sterner stuff. Hundreds volunteered to climb the hill and give the British a sound thrashing. However, just 180 expert marksmen were selected, some as young as twelve. While they set off to scale the heights, the rest kept up a barrage of fire that made the British keep their heads down. A British officer merely reported that the Boers were 'wasting ammunition'.

Ian Hamilton – later the general in charge of the disastrous Dardanelles campaign – woke Colley to warn him that a hundred Boers had reached the summit. Colley seemed unperturbed, so Hamilton returned with ever more inflated figures, eventually telling Colley that they were involved in hand-to-hand fighting. They weren't. Boer farm boys were hardly likely to take on trained soldiers who outnumbered them three to one. Instead, they took cover and picked off the British one by one.

Finally realising the danger, Colley formed up the reserve, who had, like him, been sleeping. They loosed off a volley. The Boers unsportingly ducked down, allowing the British fire to pass harmlessly over their heads. Then they got up again and fired back. Colley was hit in the head by a twelve-year-old sharpshooter and died. His men fled in panic. In all, 93 were killed, 133 wounded and 58 taken prisoner.

The British quickly made peace.

Black Week

The Boer War broke out again in 1899. That October Sir Redvers Buller was made commander-in-chief in South Africa. He was a career soldier and had been promoted effortlessly up the ranks, well beyond the level of his competence. Between 10 and 15 December 1899, he oversaw three humiliating defeats at the hands of the Boers in what the British press dubbed 'Black Week'.

Buller had already demonstrated his incompetence as a

general on the plains of Hampshire. In 1898, he had been given command of Aldershot and did not distinguish himself in the revived autumn manoeuvres, as he had no experience of commanding a force as large as a corps. Indeed, he had no experience of an independent command in the field. The manoeuvres took place only between 9 a.m. and 5 p.m., so officers had their evenings free. The men were ordered not to dive for cover in case they ruined their uniforms and they were not to dig trenches that would damage the country-side. Instead, they simply fired volleys at each other from a range of a hundred yards. This was no preparation for what the army was to face in South Africa.

The war was declared on 7 October and Buller was on his way to Cape Town a week later. By the time he arrived, Ladysmith, Mafeking and Kimberley were already under siege. There followed inept attempts to relieve them. The first was by General William Gatacre – or 'Backacher', as he was known to his troops. He aimed to first take the impor-tant railway junction at Stormberg. His plan was to take a force of more than two thousand men by train to Molteno, then make a night march to a hill known as the Kissieberg, which overlooked the Boers' position.

The troops were boarded onto the trains, but then had to wait around all day in the heat while locomotives were found. They were already tired when they arrived at Molteno. After little food and no rest, they set off. During the night march, their local guides deserted them and they became totally lost. Nevertheless, on the morning of 10 December, they found themselves at the foot of the Kissieberg. On top, the Boer picket opened fire. All the British had to do was walk around the hill and the Boers would be cut off. Instead, orders were given to storm the sheer cliff face. British artillery was brought up, but it succeeded only in shelling the infantry as it began its assault.

Unable to climb the sheer face, the British fell back, if not down. Fearing they would be cut off by a Boer counterattack, Gatacre ordered a retreat. He congratulated himself on breaking off after losing just ninety men. Then it was realised that some six hundred had not heard the order to retreat. They were now surrounded and were forced to surrender. It was a mistake any gentleman could have made, and Buller sent a telegram to Gatacre saying, 'Better luck next time.'

Meanwhile, Lord Methuen was attacking a hill near Magersfontein. Thinking the Boers were entrenched on the top, they ordered a bombardment of the heights. In fact, the Boers were entrenched at the bottom, enjoying the pyrotechnics. What's more, they were now warned of the impending attack.

Major-General Andrew Wauchope led 3,500 Highlanders into position through the pitch black of a moonless night and in torrential rain. The high iron-ore content of the surrounding hills and the thunderstorm played havoc with their compasses, and they were further hampered by rocky outcrops and thorny scrub. As dawn broke on 11 December, they were still a thousand yards short of the Boer positions.

Although it was now light, Wauchope continued his advance in a tight formation. With the Highlanders shoulder to shoulder, they were an unmissable target. At four hundred yards, an advancing British soldier tripped an alarm wire and the Boers opened up. One of the Black Watch said that is was as if 'someone had pressed a button and turned on a million electric lights'. Wauchope fell in the first volley. His dying words were recorded as, 'Don't blame me for this, lads.' Others say he merely uttered, 'What a pity.'

By then an attempt to fan out into a more open formation just added to the confusion. The only cover was provided by scrub bushes and anthills. The Highlanders were caught out in the open and stuck there throughout the heat of the day. A further artillery bombardment was concentrated on the slope of the hill, rather than the trenches at the bottom. Eventually, the Highlanders made an attempt to flee safety, only to be shot in the back by Boer sharpshooters. They had lost 210 killed, 675 wounded and 63 missing.

After collecting their dead, the British were forced to withdraw. During the retreat they were struck down by typhoid fever. Private Smith of the Black Watch summed up the pathos of their situation in verse:

> Such was the day for our regiment,
> Dread the revenge we will take.
> Dearly we paid for the blunder
> A drawing-room General's mistake.
> Why weren't we told of the trenches?
> Why weren't we told of the wire?
> Why were we marched up in column,
> May Tommy Atkins enquire . . .

As if things weren't bad enough, Sir Redvers Buller then took a hand himself and headed off to relieve Ladysmith.

On the way he ran into a Boer army under General Louis Botha that had taken up positions to the north of the Tugela River at Colenso. Buller was in too much of a hurry to bother with reconnaissance and started the battle with an artillery barrage that missed the Boers' well camouflaged trenches.

On the morning of 15 December, the British advanced across the plain to the river, even though Buller still had no idea where the Boers were. The attack was led by the 5th (Irish) Brigade under Major-General Fitzroy Hart, who had taken the precaution of giving his men half an hour's drill on the parade ground that morning. They were supposed to be heading for Bridle Drift, where the river could be forded. Instead, the local guide, who spoke no English, led them to Pont Drift in a loop in the river where they were surrounded on three sides by the Boers. Botha had given orders for his men to hold their fire until the British crossed the river, but four thousand men in close order jammed into a loop in the river a thousand yards wide was a target too good to be missed.

To escape the carnage, some of Hart's men fixed bayonets and rushed into the river, aiming to ford it and have a go at the enemy on the other side. However, the river had been swollen by recent rains and was between fifteen and twenty feet deep and a hundred yards wide. Many drowned and those who swam across were shot down by the Boers on the other side. Hart's brigade suffered 532 casualties before they could be withdrawn.

Meanwhile Major-General Henry Hildyard and the 2nd Brigade were ordered to march on the 'iron bridge', but there were two of them marked on the map. Colonel

Charles Long forged ahead of the infantry with twelve fifteen-pounder field guns and six naval guns. Although he had been ordered to stop no closer that two and a half miles from the river, he galloped up to within a thousand yards. This was within rifle range. A thousand Boer rifles opened up with withering fire. The field guns had no shields and on the flat plane there were few places to take cover. Within an hour, Long had exhausted his ammunition and his men had taken shelter in a gully.

Even though the British still had eight thousand men uncommitted, Buller tried to rescue Long's guns himself. Botha was impressed by this futile heroism. Seven Victoria Crosses were earned in the action. But eventually it proved so costly that Buller called a halt. It was just 11 a.m. when Buller decided to withdraw, leaving the wounded and the guns on the battlefield to be taken by the enemy that night. British casualties were 143 killed, 756 wounded and 220 captured. Boer losses were estimated at fifty.

Buller was replaced as commander-in-chief in South Africa by Field Marshal Lord Roberts, whose son, Lieutenant the Honourable Freddy Roberts, had been mortally wounded trying to rescue the guns at Colenso.

Hearing of the setback at Colenso, Queen Victoria dismissed the news, saying, 'We are not interested in the possibilities of defeat.'

Spion Kop

Although no longer commander-in-chief, Sir Redvers Buller remained in command in Natal, where more misfortune befell him. He was reinforced by a new division under Sir Charles Warren, the former Commissioner of the Metropolitan Police, who had failed to apprehend Jack the Ripper. Warren was also something of an eccentric. While fighting raged at Hussar Hill in February 1900, Warren entertained his men by bathing publicly. Although he was fifty-nine years old, he joined his men hauling ropes.

In another attempt to relieve Ladysmith, Buller planned to cross the Tugela River at Trichardt's Drift, capture the hills opposite and move on to the road leading to the besieged town. He put Warren in charge of this operation, although he had never commanded such a large force before and had not been on active service for fifteen years. He also had so much luggage that it took twenty-six hours to get it all across the ford. Warren personally supervised this. When the operation began, the Boers had just six hundred defenders in position to block his advance. But, by the time all this luggage was across, six thousand Boers were sitting west of Spion Kop. Skipping any reconnaissance, Warren immediately ordered an assault. The idea was that, if they could capture the peak, which stood 1,400 feet above the surrounding countryside, they could shell the Boer positions at will.

Warren picked General Talbot-Coke to lead the assault on Spion Kop. But he had only just arrived in South Africa and had an injured leg. When Buller questioned his choice, Warren chose fifty-four-year-old General Woodgate.

While twenty thousand men looked on, the Lancashire Brigade set off up Spion Kop. However, Woodgate was not as fit as he might have been, either, and halfway up the slope he had to be carried. It was dark and the peak was shrouded in fog. They found a small Boer picket, which was quickly driven off at bayonet point. The Lancashires attempted to dig in. But, between a thousand of them, they had only twenty picks and shovels. The ground was rocky and the trenches they managed to dig were no deeper than sixteen inches (40cm). Sandbags that had been prepared for the fortifications had been left at the bottom, along with the machine guns. They had taken no field telephone with them either, so it was impossible to request that they be brought up.

As dawn broke, the British found that they were not on top of the Kop at all. They only occupied a small plateau, while the Boers held the higher ground on three sides of them. The Boers were able to fire down on them from the surrounding peaks, and the shallow trenches they had dug afforded them no protection.

Unaware of the true situation, the hapless Warren believed that the assault on Spion Kop had been a great success and, when Winston Churchill, who was covering the campaign as a war correspondent, pointed out that the men were trapped, he flew into a rage and threatened to have Churchill arrested. In fact, the situation could have been saved if reinforcements had been sent immediately. Warren did nothing.

The Boers began to bombard the British trenches with artillery and sent more men to take flanking positions. However, the British managed to hold off a ferocious frontal assault.

By this time Woodgate was dead. Command changed

from hand to hand until it passed to Colonel Alexander Thorneycroft. The first runner sent to tell Thorneycroft that he was now a brigadier was shot dead before he could pass on the news.

Some of the Lancashire Fusiliers tried to surrender. Thorneycroft prevented this, shouting at the Boers who advanced to round up prisoners, 'I'm the commandant here; take your men back to hell, sir! I allow no surrenders.'

As darkness fell, the Boers began to retreat. Botha persuaded them to stay, but they did not even reoccupy their earlier positions. The battle could then have been won then, had Thorneycroft known it. But in the morning, after hearing nothing from Warren and running short of water and ammunition, he withdrew. As the survivors set off down the slope, they met reinforcements on their way up. But it was too late, and the Boer generals were surprised to see their men on top of Spion Kop the next day. The British suffered 1,493 casualties, 243 of whom were dead. Many were buried where they fell in the trenches on top of the Kop. The Boers suffered 335 casualties, 68 dead.

The British pulled back across the Tugela, but the Boers were too weak to press home their success. Buller wrote to his wife, 'Old Warren is a duffer and lost me a good chance.'

Warren was sent back to England, where he was immediately promoted general. He later became a leading light in the Boy Scouts. It was Buller who was blamed for the catastrophe at Spion Kop and was known, from then on, as 'Sir Reverse Buller'. To be fair, Buller did manage to rally his troops and relieved Ladysmith four weeks later.

Several football stadiums adopted the name 'Spion Kop',

or 'the Kop', as name for their banked stands. The most famous is in Liverpool FC's Anfield ground.

Machine-gun madness

The man generally thought to be responsible for much of the senseless slaughter of the First World War was Sir Douglas Haig, a former cavalry officer who was so well prepared for the conditions on the Western Front that he said in 1915, 'The machine gun is a much-overrated weapon; two per battalion is more than sufficient.'

Haig was with the cavalry when they made their last great charge at the Battle of Omdurman in the Sudan in 1898. It was said that he was a cavalry man to the bottom of his boots. Others said, unkindly, that he was bright only to the *top* of his boots. By 1914, the machine gun had been in service with the British Army for over thirty years, but it was thought to be useful only for mowing down natives in colonial wars. The British thought it unsporting to use it against other Europeans.

Militarily, the machine gun was seen as a defensive weapon when the British ethos of the day promoted 'up and at 'em' offensive warfare. Because the machine gun was heavy and used from a static emplacement, it was thought that it would slow down any infantry advance and inhibit the mobility of an army as a whole. Plainly the British had learnt nothing from the Boer War, where they had lost action after action against the concentrated fire of Boer riflemen. Military theorists who argued that the superior firepower of the machine gun could be used in offensive actions were studiously ignored.

Although machine guns were available at the beginning of the First World War, the commander-in-chief Sir John French and Douglas Haig refused to release men to train on them. By February 1915, 890 machine guns were lying idle in France for want of men who could use them. However, when David Lloyd George became Minister of Munitions later that year, he increased the allocation to sixteen per battalion. The problem was that the manufacturers could not keep up with the orders. While the Germans and French had been turning out hundreds of machine guns between 1904 and 1914 in preparation for war, Vickers had been called on to produce only eleven a year. Now they were being ordered in their thousands.

Tanks, but no tanks

The development of the tank broke the deadlock of trench warfare and proved the war-winning weapon in 1918, but cavalrymen such as Douglas Haig saw no future for it. Although the last major cavalry engagement in Western Europe had taken place during the Franco-Prussian War in

1870, horsemen saw its use against the Turks in Palestine in 1917 as proof that it had a future role.

At the end of the First World War, tank production ceased. Defence cuts in 1922 left the British Army with just six tank battalions, while there were still twenty cavalry regiments. By 1929, £72,000 a year was being spent on tanks and motorised vehicles, while £607,000 was being spent on fodder for horses.

After the war, Lieutenant-Colonel John Frederic Charles 'Boney' Fuller, who had led the first major breakthrough by tanks at the Battle of Cambrai in 1917, began writing books about the future of tank warfare. The chief of the Imperial General Staff, Sir Archibald Montgomery Massingberd, refused to read them and dismissed them out of hand. Eventually, he had to establish the 1st Tank Brigade as a permanent formation in 1933.

Basil Liddell Hart wrote a series of articles that advocated the coordination of tanks and aircraft, only to be told by General Sir James Edmonds that the tank had had its day. However, in Germany someone was listening to what Fuller and Liddell Hart had to say. His name was Heinz Guderian and he used their work in the development of the *blitzkrieg*.

Tanked it

Sir Douglas Haig may have had good reason for his assessment of the tank. During the First World War, they could be a mixed blessing. On 15 September 1916, it was reported that two tanks had broken through the German lines and taken the village of Flers. However, the press did not

mention that one of the tanks had lost its bearings. It mistook a British trench for a German one and machine-gunned the 9th Norfolk Regiment, who were preparing to go over the top. It was only when an officer leapt up waving his arms and shouting 'Stop!' that the tank crew, peering through the narrow slits in the armour, realised their mistake and broke off. The rest of the Norfolks were cut down later that day by the occupants of the German trenches, which had been the tank's original objective.

Hunter-Bunter

Major-General A.G. Hunter-Weston is known to historians as the 'Butcher of Helles' for his disastrous command of the British forces at Gallipoli in 1915. But his men called him 'Hunter-Bunter' because his considerable girth reminded them of the overweight schoolboy Billy Bunter, hero of the *Magnet* comic.

At Cape Helles he landed with the elite 29th ('Incomparable') Division, sustaining heavy casualties. 'Casualties? What do I care for casualties?' he said. He had already warned his men that they must expect 'heavy losses by bullets, by shells, by mines and by drowning'. He was right. There was a bloodbath.

Once ashore, he encouraged his men further, telling them that 'every man must die at his post rather than retire'.

This was entirely unnecessary, as the Turks had withdrawn in the face of the massive British landings. However, due to Hunter-Weston's mismanagement, the British did not exploit the situation.

Despite happily sacrificing the 29th, Hunter-Weston was given command of the Eighth Corps. He continued to order frontal assaults in broad daylight, abandoning any attempt at surprise. This ensured maximum casualties. When told that one brigade had lost 1,300 men, he said he was delighted to have 'blooded the pups'.

After four months, Hunter-Weston collapsed with sun-stroke and was invalided home, where he was promptly knighted.

Bay bunglers

As if Hunter-Weston had not ballsed up the Gallipoli landings enough, the Minister of War, Lord Kitchener, sent another ageing buffoon, the sixty-one-year-old Lieutenant-General Sir Frederick Stopford, to make further landings at Suvla Bay in August 1915. Not only was Stopford incompetent, he surrounded himself with other bunglers. One of his divisional commanders, Major-General Hammersley, had recently suffered a nervous breakdown. At the first sound of gunfire, he lay on the floor of his tent with his hands over his head. According to an official report into the fiasco, Hammersley's orders were 'confused and the work of his staff defective', while the senior brigade commander, General Sitwell, 'did not, in our opinion, show sufficient energy and decision'.

The plan was simple. Twenty-two thousand men would be landed against minimal Turkish opposition. They would march four miles inland and occupy the heights, allowing the ANZAC and other British troops landed in April to break out of their beachheads. Surprise would be the key.

Stopford was in poor health and had never held a field command before. While his men went ashore, Stopford had a nap on his yacht. Meanwhile, some of the destroyers towing the lighters – flat-bottomed barges – carrying the troops anchored a mile from the designated beach and landed the men there. Some of the lighters ended up grounded on shoals; others found themselves at the bottom of sheer cliffs. The lighter carrying the water supply for two divisions ran aground a hundred yards from shore, leaving them without water for twenty-four hours. A German cavalry officer observing the landings from the height said the situation was so confused that it looked as if someone had disturbed an anthill.

When Stopford awoke, he found his men safely ashore. But, instead of rapidly mounting an assault on his objective, he decided that his men needed rest, more water and artillery support before they could progress inland. He later told the enquiry that he assumed that the hills were 'strongly entrenched'. In fact, his twenty-two battalions faced just fifteen hundred men.

While Hammersley was too ill to progress and Sitwell too exhausted, another divisional commander, Lieutenant-General Sir Bryan Mahon, threw a tantrum, considering himself too senior to command a mere division. When nine of the twelve brigades had been reallocated, he refused to attack a hill occupied by just seven hundred Turks with his remaining three thousand men, and resigned in the middle of the battle. He went on to become the commander-in-chief in Ireland in the run-up to the Anglo-Irish War.

The British commander in the Dardanelles, Sir Ian Hamilton, grew worried that nothing was happening at Suvla Bay. Aerial reconnaissance reported no strong Turkish forces in the area, but Stopford seemed to be making no progress towards the hills. Hamilton sent two aides to find out what was going on. They found a scene that looked like 'August Bank Holiday in England' with men bathing and lounging on the beach. Despite their urging, Stopford could not be persuaded to seize the initiative – and the hills.

Then Hamilton himself turned up. He found Stopford resting on his yacht, saying his leg was too painful to go ashore. But if Hamilton insisted on an attack, he should go ashore himself and talk to the divisional commanders.

By this time, some British troops, on their own initiative, had occupied one of the hills. They were recalled to form up on the beach. The Turks then moved in and took over their positions.

When Stopford eventually came ashore the next day, he stopped on the beach to have a bombproof shelter built for him and his staff. By then six thousand British troops were being held off by eight hundred Turks.

'We are being held up by three men,' a young officer told Hamilton. 'There is one little man with a white beard, one man in a blue coat and one boy in shirt sleeves.'

Soon, Mustapha Kemal turned up, reinforcing the Turkish defenders. Before the British force was evacuated in December, eight thousand were dead. Stopford had been dismissed after just nine days. He returned to his duties as lieutenant of the Tower of London, a post he had held before the war, and was made a Knight Commander of the Order of the Bath.

Down the Loos

On 25 September 1915, Douglas Haig was ordered to take the French town of Loos by the British commander-in-chief Sir John French. But there was a shortage of heavy guns, so Haig decided to use chlorine gas. This was generally considered unsporting by the British, but the Germans had demonstrated that they were not going to 'play the game' when they had first used poison gas that April. It was all the more ironic that Haig was suffering from a mild attack of asthma at the time.

Haig delayed the attack for nine minutes to be sure that the wind was blowing in the right direction. As it was, the dense clouds of yellowy green gas billowed out into no-man's-land, where it stopped. In some places, it blew back into the British trenches, where some men had removed their gas masks because they could not see through the fogged-up eyepieces or found they could not breathe.

When the men did go over the top, they found themselves in an impenetrable fog of chlorine gas. While some objectives were achieved, losses were devastating, so Haig decided to call in reserves. He asked French for General

Haking's XI Corps, which included two divisions of raw recruits fresh from England. Haig said that the 'enthusiasm of ignorance' would help them tear through the German lines. Besides, Haig reassured Haking that the Germans were already beaten and his men would be pursuing an enemy in full retreat.

When the 21st and 24th Divisions arrived on the front on the night of 25 September, they had been marching through the autumn rain for eighteen hours without food. They had no proper maps and no knowledge of the area. At one point they were stopped by a military policeman, because they did not have the proper passes. With no artillery support and no gas, they were sent into action the following morning. The Germans saw ten lines of men a thousand abreast proceeding slowly across no-man's-land led by officers on horseback. For the machine-gunners they presented an unmissable target. Riflemen climbed out of their trenches and stood on the parapets to make sure every bullet counted.

Nearing the German trenches, the British came across an unbroken field of barbed wire nineteen feet thick. Their puny clippers could not cut it. Men tore at the wire with their bare hands while they were shot down. Others ran up and down looking for a place where the wire was broken, but there was no way through.

The scale of the massacre was so horrendous that the Germans stopped firing when the remnants of the two divisions retreated. Of the 10,000 who had attacked, 385 officers and 7,861 men were listed as casualties. The Germans lost not a single man. By 28 September, the British were back at their starting point, after losing over 20,000 men, including three divisional commanders.

Haig ordered another offensive on 13 October, which failed due to a shortage of hand grenades. A third offensive on 7 November was called off due to heavy rain. Despite this disaster, Haig replaced French as commander-in-chief, while French was made first Earl of Ypres – after commanding the first two battles of Ypres, where more than 117,000 men were lost.

A walk on the wild side

On the first day of the Battle of the Somme, 1 July 1916, Haig told his men that the initial artillery bombardment would cut the barbed wire protecting the German trenches allowing his cavalry to gallop through. Morale was so high that one brigadier-general told his men that they could go over the top carrying walking sticks. They would not need their rifles. Some officers took him at his word. Captain Wilfred Nevill of the East Surrey Regiment headed out into no-man's-land kicking a football. He was killed instantly.

The bombardment would be so heavy that the 16th Battalion of the Northumberland Fusiliers – also known as the Newcastle Commercials, a 'pals' battalion – were told that they would find all the Germans dead; not even rats would survive. However, the beastly Germans rather unsportingly took shelter in concrete bunkers.

The Sherwood Foresters were told, 'You will meet nothing but dead and wounded Germans . . . The field kitchens will follow you and give you a good meal.'

The King's Own Yorkshire Rifles' instructions were, 'When you go over the top, you can slope arms, light up your pipes and cigarettes, and march all the way to Pozières before meeting any live Germans.'

French soldiers crossed no-man's-land in bunches, dodging from shell hole to shell hole, but the British on the Somme were mainly Kitchener's 'New Army', fresh volunteers who had not seen action before. Carrying seventy pounds of kit, they were ordered to walk upright, in four ranks, a yard or so from their neighbours, at walking pace to prevent them panicking and diving for cover. The Germans could not believe their eyes. One said, 'The English came walking, as though they were going to the theatre or as though they were on a parade ground. We felt they were mad. Our orders were given in complete calm and every man took careful aim to avoid wasting ammunition.'

Another said, 'When the English started advancing we were very worried. They looked as though they must overrun our trenches. We were very surprised to see them walking, we had never seen that before. I could see them everywhere. There were hundreds. The officers were in front. I noticed one of them walking calmly, carrying a walking stick. When we started firing, we just had to load and reload. They went down in their hundreds. You didn't have to aim, we just fired into them. If only they had run, they would have over-whelmed us.'

A French observer compared the advance to the charge of the Light Brigade. Sir Henry Rawlinson, commanding the Fourth Army on the Somme, thought this approach entirely appropriate, comparing the area to the army training ground on Salisbury Plain 'with large open rolling features, and any number of partridges which we were not allowed to shoot'.

The British had been to great lengths to keep their plans for an offensive secret. They sent up the Royal Flying Corps to see off German reconnaissance planes. However, British newspapers reported that munitions workers had had their Whitsun leave cancelled, so it was obvious that something was afoot. It was easy to tell where, as the Royal Flying Corps concentrated their efforts in the area along the Somme. A week-long artillery barrage preceded the attack.

Rawlinson had called up 1,437 guns to pound a 15-mile front to cut the wire and destroy the German defences. However, only 467 of the artillery pieces were heavy guns, and just 34 of 9.2-inch calibre or more. Two-thirds of the shells contained shrapnel, which was deadly to men caught out in the open but ineffective against barbed wire coiled so thick that, in some places, it obscured the light.

The Germans had had two years to prepare their bunkers along the Somme, some of which were thirty feet deep. Of the twelve thousand tons of explosives fired by the British, only nine hundred tons were high explosive of the type needed to smash concrete bunkers. The British wire cutters were too puny to cut the wire and the Tommies milled about waiting to be shot. In the few places where the wire *had* been cut, things were no better. It simply bunched the men together, making them an easier target.

Although Hunter-Weston was called a 'butcher' by the 29th, after a year's home leave he was given command of the Eighth Corps again, this time in France. At the Battle of the Somme, he told his men that bombardment had cut the wire, when they could see with their own eyes that it had not. He ordered the artillery to stop firing ten minutes before his men went over the top, giving the Germans plenty of time to emerge and set up their 'much-overrated' machine guns. The 29th were caught in the open and machine-gunned to a man. On 1 July 1916, the Eighth Corps alone suffered 14,581 casualties and took no enemy positions. The meagre gains made were abandoned within a day of capture. Hunter-Weston blamed the artillery for stopping their barrage too early, although he had given the order himself.

By nightfall, the British lost 57,470 of their 120,000 men. Of the 21,000 killed, most died within the first thirty minutes. The 10th West Yorks were wiped out in less than a minute. No one was left alive to relate the fate of the 1st Hampshires. But it was all rather splendid. Brigadier-General Rees, commanding the 94th Infantry Brigade, said, 'They advanced line after line, dressed as if on parade, and not a man shirked going through the extremely heavy barrage, or facing the machine-gun fire that finally wiped them out . . . I have never seen such a magnificent display of gallantry, discipline and determination. The reports I have had from the very few survivors of this marvellous advance bear out what I saw . . . that hardly a man of ours got to the German front line.'

This did not stop Rawlinson sending in a second wave, again at walking pace, when the first had been slaughtered.

For a meagre capture of territory on one part of the front, the British army suffered greater casualties than on any other day in its history – more than the entire Crimean War, Boer War and Korean War put together. However, that evening Haig summed up by saying, 'The general situation was favourable.' The Somme campaign continued for another five months, eventually costing Haig's armies 420,000 casualties while still falling short of his objectives for the first day. Haig, naturally, was promoted to field marshal and, while the French went on the defensive, awaiting the arrival of the Americans, Haig began another, purely British, offensive the following year.

After the war, Rawlinson was given a vote of thanks by Parliament and made a baron. Hunter-Weston had become an MP and died after falling from a turret at his home in Hunterston in 1940.

Drowning in mud

Flanders was a marshland that had been reclaimed over the centuries. In 1917, Field Marshal Douglas Haig was warned that a heavy bombardment of the area around Ypres was turning the land back into a swamp. He went ahead and ordered an offensive there anyway. It came as no surprise to the Germans. The night before the attack, General William

Robertson said, 'Everybody in my hotel knows the date of the offensive down to the lift boy.'

The offensive began with a fortnight's intensive bombardment with 4.5 million shells being fired from three thousand guns and five tons of high explosive falling on every square yard of the front. This did no damage to the Germans, as they had pulled back. But it did smash the drainage system and the heavy rain predicted by the Meteorological Office turned the landscape into a sea of mud. The newly introduced tanks became stuck and men drowned. Others presented easy targets to the German machine-gunners perched on top of their concrete bunkers as they advanced along narrow duckboards. Meanwhile, the Germans managed to site their artillery on a firm footing on the few remaining ridges. Haig and his staff remained in a chateau well behind in the lines and did not bother to witness the devastation he had caused. In briefings, he spoke as if the attack had taken place in high summer.

With the imminent capitulation of Russia freeing up twenty divisions to be sent to the Western Front, Haig was ordered to keep casualties to the minimum. So he cooked the books, sending the wounded to VD clinics or back to the front. The Australians suffered a casualty rate of 60 per cent. Half the Canadian guns were underwater, clogged with mud or missing somewhere under the quagmire. Two companies of Canadians were fired on by British guns who were supposed to be supporting them. The survivors ran back from the slaughter ahead, and were shot down by the British companies following them. When the Canadian Prime Minister Robert Borden heard about his, he grabbed

Lloyd George by the lapels at a meeting of the War Cabinet and shook him in fury.

Incessant rain in October drowned the guns. One gunner reported that, every time he fired his gun, the breach went underwater. When Haig's artillery adviser, Colonel Rawlins, warned his commander that, at that rate, there would be no guns left for 1918, Haig ordered him to leave the room. When Brigadier-General James Edmonds agreed with Rawlins, Haig said, 'You go, too.'

British losses were put at 325,000 for an advance of five miles – that's less than an inch per man. Five months later the Germans regained their lost ground without resistance.

After the war, Haig was made an earl. He is also remembered for his promotion of army dentistry. He had suffered from toothache during the Battle of Ypres and sent to Paris for a dentist. Fearing that his men may suffer the same discomfort, he employed dozens of them. By the end of the war, there were 831 dentists working for the British Army and the Army Dental Corps was formed in 1921.

CHAPTER THREE

Misguided Manoeuvres

I T IS EASY TO LOOK back over the years with the benefit of hindsight and mock the military mistakes of our forebears. However, there have been some monumental misjudgements that, were it not for the thousands who paid with their lives, border on the comical.

Balls-up at Bannockburn

Edward II was an immensely unpopular king over his relationship with his favourite Piers Gaveston, who was thought to be his lover. In 1312, the barons turned against Edward, seized Gaveston and executed him. In an attempt to restore his authority, Edward sought to emulate his father, Edward I, famed as the 'Hammer of the Scots' for his invasions of Scotland in 1296 and 1298.

In 1314, the few remaining English troops in Scotland were under siege in Stirling Castle. The English governor of Stirling Castle, Sir Philip Mowbray, made a pact with the besiegers. If no relief came by midsummer, he would surrender the castle. If relief arrived, the Scots would withdraw – so there was no need for any fighting. But Edward II had no intention of being bound by this agreement. As he led his troops north, he intended not just to relieve Stirling Castle, but to destroy the Scottish army in the field and restore English rule to Scotland.

Edward was still so unpopular in England that only three of his earls supported him and supplied only the minimum of mounted troops. Nevertheless, the English army outnumbered the Scots by at least two to one, and probably four to one. But Edward made almost every mistake a military commander could make.

When he arrived in sight of Stirling Castle, Sir Philip Mowbray was given safe conduct to visit his camp and urged Edward to stay his hand, believing that the Scots would withdraw as they had promised. Edward refused to listen. Mowbray also warned Edward not to accept battle on a low-lying area of bog along a tidal estuary that was unsuited to heavy cavalry. Again, Edward would not listen.

Next, Edward confused the chain of command, replacing the old and experienced Constable of England, Humphrey de Bohun, Earl of Hereford, with his hot-headed young rival Gilbert de Clare, Earl of Gloucester, for the duration of the battle. Enmity between the two spread confusion throughout the army before the battle had even begun. As soon as they saw the Scots, they raced towards them, each determined to strike the first blow.

Ahead of the pack was Hereford's nephew, Henry de Bohun. Spotting the Scottish king Robert the Bruce

mounted on a small palfrey and wearing no armour, de Bohun lowered his lance and charged. Bruce held his ground as the great warhorse thundered towards him.

Then, at the last moment, he raised his battleaxe and struck de Bohun such a blow that it split his helmet and his head. The Scottish commanders were furious that Bruce had taken such a risk, but it gave a huge boost to Scottish morale, while crushing that of the English. Bruce was only sorry that he had broken his favourite battleaxe.

Another division of cavalry under Henry de Beaumont tried to outflank the Scots but came up against a phalanx of pikemen under Sir Thomas Grey. Grey told Beaumont that he could withdraw unmolested. This was an offer that no self-respecting knight could accept. Instead, Beaumont charged. With no archers to cut the pikemen down, Beaumont's knights were quickly impaled.

More English knights attacked another Scottish phalanx of pikemen under Robert the Bruce's brother Edward, Earl of Moray. Again, no English archers were on hand and the English knights were quickly skewered. By evening the English were despondent. But worse was to come. Edward ordered his knights to cross the Bannock Burn and make their camp there. But the ground was so swampy there that they had to use tables and doors from the village nearby to take the weight of the horses. Meanwhile, the infantry, who had had little to do so far, got drunk. And no one slept, expecting an attack by the Scots any moment.

As it was, Bruce was considering withdrawing and resorting to guerrilla warfare after having succeeded in giving the English a bloody nose. However, that night one of Edward's knights, Sir Alexander Seton, a landowner from Lothian, defected. This convinced Bruce that English morale was shattered and he should fight on.

The following day, the English knights found it impossible to find their footing. When they did succeed in finding firmer ground, they were still confined between Bannock Burn and the estuary of the River Forth. On such a narrow front, it was impossible to mount a cavalry charge. Belatedly, the English archers were brought into play. But they risked hitting the densely packed horsemen, who were also in danger of being crushed or suffocated. But, before the archers could do much damage to the Scottish pikemen, they were driven off by light horse under Sir Robert Keith.

Some five hundred knights led Edward to safety away from the battlefield. Seeing the king fleeing, the English army broke. The Scottish camp followers then picked up weapons and pitched in. The English were trapped and slaughtered. Pushed back, many were drowned in the Burn. More were killed by the pursuing army and the inhabitants of the countryside as they fled back towards the border. Accurate casualty figures are impossible to come by, but it is thought that fewer than a third of the English foot soldiers survived. Sixty barons and bannerets, and many scores of English knights, perished. The Scots lost just two knights, along with numerous pikemen. It was the greatest defeat an

English king had suffered since the Battle of Hastings, and Scotland was, once again, free.

The disaster had scarcely improved Edward's standing. He then did himself no favours by taking two more favourites, a father and son both named Hugh le Despenser. Fed up with his infidelity, Edward's wife, Isabella, became the mistress of the exiled knight Roger Mortimer. Isabella and Mortimer invaded, executed the Despensers and imprisoned Edward. Later he was found dead in his cell after, it was rumoured, a red-hot poker had been shoved up 'those parts in which he had been wont to take his vicious pleasure'.

However, under Edward II's successor, his son Edward III, the English finally mastered the use of archers and routed the Scots at the Battle of Halidon Hill in 1333.

The Battle of the Yellow Ford

In England's numerous attempts to subdue Ireland, its biggest defeat came at the Battle of the Yellow Ford in 1598. In Tudor times, the English pursued the disastrous policy of building small enclaves throughout rural Ireland. These isolated garrisons were difficult to defend and supply. One of them was built on the River Blackwater, five miles northwest of Armagh. Almost immediately, it was besieged by Hugh O'Neill, Earl of Tyrone, a Gaelic Ulsterman who grew up in London.

The fort was held by 150 men under Captain Thomas Williams. They had to fight their way out of the fort to get fresh water or firewood and, in the winter of 1597, much of the earthworks were washed away by a flood. But Tyrone refused to take the fort, as it was a useful bait to lure in English soldiers sent to reprovision it. Nor would the English relinquish this strategic liability for fear of losing face.

In August 1598 a resupply column set out from Armagh under Sir Henry Bagenal, Tyrone's brother-in-law, who had already commanded a series of military disasters in Ireland. He had three hundred horse and four thousand foot – a considerable force in those days. However, many of the infantrymen were raw recruits who sold their arms and uniforms as soon as they were given them and deserted at the first opportunity.

The infantry were draw up into regiments, marching a hundred yards apart. They were shot at by the Irish hidden in woods to the flanks. Pits had been dug to thwart any counterattack by the cavalry. Under constant harassment, the gap between the regiments grew longer and longer. Then the supply wagons got stuck in the bogs and the column broke into three sections, each attacked by the Irish.

The vanguard came up against a trench a mile long filled with water and thorns, which was flanked by bogs. One regiment got across, but were forced back by Tyrone's men into the ditch. Bagenal tried to rally his troops and, momentarily, raised his visor – only to be shot in the face. With their commander dead, the English fled back to Armagh. They had lost twenty-five officers and eight hundred men, with another four hundred wounded.

The English defeat sparked an uprising across Ireland. Coming to their aid, four thousand Spanish troops landed at Kinsale in 1601. They were surrounded, and Tyrone suffered a stinging defeat attempting to raise the siege. He finally surrendered on 30 March 1803, six days after the death of Elizabeth I. Elizabeth's successor, James I of England, allowed Tyrone to keep most of his land, but he could not

stand bending his knee to the British. In 1607, he set out for Spain with a hundred northern chieftains. Blown off course, they landed in the Netherlands and made their way to Rome. The so-called 'flight of the earls' marked the end of Gaelic Ulster.

Marston MoorRight Royal screw-up

The impatience of Royalist commander Lord John Byron cost King Charles I the Battle of Marston Moor in 1644, the first major Royalist defeat in the Civil War. Byron's cavalry on the Royalist right wing were clearly outnumbered two to one by Oliver Cromwell's cavalry on the Parliamentarians' left. So Prince Rupert, commanding the king's army, told Byron to hold his position. There was an area of marshy ground in front of him and a ditch. This would slow Parliamentarian cavalry and they would be thinned by muskets and a field battery on the flank.

But, as the Cromwell's men galloped towards him, Byron forgot his orders and charged. Consequently, it was the Royalist cavalry that were slowed by the marshy ground and the ditch. They blocked the fire of the battery and scattered the musketeers who were to have cut down the Roundheads. As a result, they were destroyed by the superior force. Cromwell then rode around the back of Rupert's army, encircling the centre and attacking the left wing from behind.

The Royalists lost between three and four thousand killed. Many more were taken prisoner along with their cannons. York fell. The king lost control of the North and Cromwell became Parliament's leading general.

Amphibious antics

After his victory in the Civil War and the First Anglo-Dutch War, Oliver Cromwell came up with his Western Design to rob Catholic Spain of its colonies in the West Indies. The prize was the Hispaniola, the island that since the Treaty of Ryswick in 1697 has been divided between French controlled Saint-Domingue and Spanish port that became the Dominican Republic. In command of the expedition was forty-two-year-old veteran General Robert Venables and Admiral William Penn – father of the William Penn who founded Pennsylvania, whom the diarist and naval administrator Samuel Pepys described as 'as false a fellow as ever was born'. Generally dividing the command of an expedition is a recipe for disaster. Cromwell compounded this danger by appointing another three commissioners to oversee the operation. One of them was Greg Butler, a notoriously drunken Irishman.

Soldiers who had survived in the Civil War were not eager to travel abroad for more adventure and the men who signed up were described as 'hectors, knights of the blade, with common cheats, thieves, cutpurses, and such like lewd persons, who had long lived by sleight of hand, and dexterity of it, and were now making a fair progress into Newgate, from whence they were to proceed towards Tyburn . . . but considering the dangerousness of that passage, very politely directed their courage another way, and became soldiers for the state'.

The navy had this untrained rabble boarded on their transports before Venables even had a chance to count them, let alone inspect them. Venables also complained that the navy had kept the best supplies for themselves. Meanwhile, he insisted on taking with him his new young wife – a move guaranteed not to endear him to men who had had to leave their wives behind.

Penn and Venables left Portsmouth on 25 December 1654 with the largest armada then to leave English waters eager to get their hands on Spanish gold. This was no secret. The Spanish knew where they were headed. However, all they did to reinforce the island was to send two hundred musketeers and a new governor, the Count of Penalva. Nevertheless, Venables did not feel that the 2,500 men he had on board were enough, so when they reached Barbados he recruited 3,000 more. These men were largely criminals transported to the island's plantations as indentured labour and would do anything to escape the island. Certainly, they were no better than their counterparts from England.

To arm these men, muskets had to be solicited from the planters, and the blacksmiths' shops of Barbados were employed turning out pikes. There was enough metal available to fashion 2,500 pike heads, but no suitable wood was found to make the shafts. So the heads had to be mounted on flimsy 'cabbage stalks' that would snap if ever put to the test in combat.

Commissioner Butler went ashore at the island of St Kitts, which was then a condominium split between the British and the French. As Britain was not at war with the French at the time, Butler thought he ought to pay a courtesy call on the French authorities. He arrived drunk, fell off his horse and vomited. On the island, he managed to recruit another 380 undesirables, putting a further strain on the inadequate supplies the convoy had brought with it.

The defences of Santo Domingo, capital of Hispaniola, were puny. It was easily in range of naval bombardment and manned by a small garrison. Venables suggested they make a direct assault on the town. Penn insisted that the main force be landed six miles to the west at the mouth of a river by Rear Admiral William Goodson, while a smaller force made a diversionary landing to the east.

Goodson and Venables set off west. It was only when they were well past the beach where they had intended to land that they discovered they had left the pilot behind. They had to land some thirty miles downwind, two days' march from Santo Domingo. At their first meal break, the soldiers discovered they had little water, over-salted meat and mouldy bread. Some men drank water they found in ditches and came down with the 'bloody flux' – dysentery. Others suffered the same effect from eating the local fruit and were forced to continue the march wearing no trousers. Meanwhile the Spanish offered African slaves and freed Creoles a bounty for every English head they collected and the column was ambushed around every bend.

They happened on an Irishman who might have been useful as a guide. But Venables had fought alongside Cromwell in Ireland. He did not trust the Irish and had the man hanged. Along the way, Venables's men came across a statue of the Madonna – a symbol of Popery – which they pelted with oranges and smashed. The locals were outraged and refused them any assistance.

On day two of the march, Venables's men were rattled when they saw a soldier up ahead. He turned out to be English, one of the party that was supposed to have been landed to the east of Santo Domingo under Commissioner Butler. The crew of their boats had also got lost and they were landed in the very place where Venables was supposed to have made landfall.

Soon after, the combined force walked straight into a Spanish ambush. The raw English recruits turned and ran. Venables hid behind a tree. Having lost face, he headed back to the fleet, saying he was going to consult Admiral Penn. While he consoled himself with his wife, his men were left without food or shelter. What food did get out to them had been taken, by mistake, from the condemned store in Barbados and several men died of food poisoning. Meanwhile, foot soldiers foraged for dogs and cats, while cavalrymen slaughtered their mounts.

An account of the condition of the troops comes from Henry Whistler's *A Journal of Admiral Penn's Expedition to the West Indies in 1654–55*. It says,

> General Venables, being aboard of our ships, and having a good ship under him and his wife to lie by his side, did not feel the hardship of the soldiers that did lie on the sand until the rain did wash it from under them, and having little or no victuals, and nothing to drink but water . . . and the abundance of fruit that they did eat, and lying in the rain did cause most of them to have the bloody flux, and now their hearts were gone out of their doublets into their breeches, and was nothing but shitting, for they were in a very sad condition.

In the rain, their biscuits rotted and they could not keep their powder dry.

Venables's return to the flagship did nothing to heal the rift with Penn. When Penn offered to send naval supplies to his men – or use his sailors to storm Santo Domingo – Venables testily declined. He returned to land determined to salve his honour by taking Santo Domingo by storm. He ordered his men to march on the city, where he intended to destroy the Spanish in front of the city walls. However, if he had simply sent a man to reconnoitre he would have discovered that the far side of the city was not protected by walls at all, only hedges.

The British full-frontal attack fell into Penalva's hands. He had put his musketeers into trenches alongside the road. The assault force was headed by Adjutant-General Jackson.

He put his worst men at the front of the column, instead of the best, while stationing himself at the back. Before they ever reached the ambush, the men were fainting from the heat. When the bullets began to fly, they turned and ran, accompanied by Adjutant-General Jackson himself. Two English officers drew their swords and tried to stop them. They were overrun.

Four hundred men lay dead, their heads quickly culled by the bounty hunters, and the British regimental standards were paraded through the streets of Santo Domingo. Venables ordered his men back to the beaches. Jackson was court-martialled. His sword was broken over his head and he was handed over to the navy to swab decks.

The fleet sailed for the altogether easier target of Jamaica. Even there, the troops fled when they heard rustling in the undergrowth, fearing more headhunters. It turned out that the rustling was caused by land crabs. Jamaica was defended by two hundred men with three cannons, commanded by Don Juan Ramirez de Orellana, who was swathed from head to foot in bandages because of an unfortunate skin condition and had to be carried everywhere on a litter. Even Venables and Penn could defeat him, and Jamaica was taken for the Commonwealth.

Nevertheless, Cromwell was not best pleased when the fleet returned to England. Venables and Penn were locked in the Tower in chains. When Venables was released, he had to suffer the tongue of his wife, who lambasted him for his failure.

'The success was very ill,' she said, 'for the work of God was not like to be done by the Devil's instruments. A wicked army it was, and sent out without arms or provisions.'

However, he found consolation in country pursuits. In 1662, he published *The Experienced Angler, or, Angling Improved*, which went through five editions in his lifetime.

Penn took to the sea again in the Restoration fleet sent to bring Charles II home in 1660 and was knighted. The king found himself in debt to Penn. As payment he signed the charter giving lands in the American colonies to his son William. Although, as a Quaker, William Penn did not approve of his father's military career, he named Pennsylvania after him.

Cock-up in Canada

During the War of 1812, fifty-eight-year-old US veteran of the War of Independence William Hull was sent to invade Canada. His first task was a two-hundred-mile march from Cincinnati to Detroit through Indian country. Incredibly, he took his daughter and her two young children with him. There were no roads. It rained incessantly and they were besieged by mosquitoes and blackfly.

Reaching the Maumee River that runs into Lake Erie, Hull commandeered a schooner to carry their baggage to Detroit. It was only after the schooner had left that Hull received, via regular post, the official notification from the Secretary of State that war had been declared. The schooner was seized by the British as it passed Fort Malden. On board was a chest containing the army muster rolls, Hull's orders and plans of the campaign.

When Hull reached Fort Malden, the British garrison was about to leave. But, as Hull showed no sign of attacking, it held on and was soon reinforced by an eighteen-gun British man-of-war. His opponent, General Isaac Brock, sent more troops and spread the word that more than six thousand Indian allies of the British were on their way. He also dressed locals in red tunics so it would appear that they were regular soldiers. Hull retreated back across the river to Detroit. There, he retired to his room and spoke to no one for four days. Meanwhile, two attempts to relieve Hull were ambushed by the British and their Shawnee allies.

Brock then offered to parley, turning up with six hundred Indians wearing war paint.

'It is far from my inclination to join in a war of extermination,' he said, 'but you must be aware that the numerous body of Indians who have attached themselves to my troops will be beyond my control the moment the contest commences.'

Nevertheless, Hull refused to surrender and placed cannons packed with grapeshot outside the stockade. But, when the British advanced, he ordered his men back into the fort. A British shell then burst inside the fort, causing several casualties. Without firing a shot in return, Hull gave up, also surrendering a column of 350 and two of his best commanders who had been out looking for help. They were disarmed when they returned. It was only later that Hull discovered his men outnumbered the enemy – even counting the Indians – by about two to one.

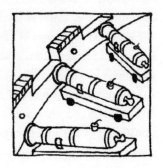

On his return from captivity, Hull was court-martialled and sentenced to be shot. He was reprieved by President James Madison and spent the rest of his life writing books in an effort to clear his name.

Brock's plans to continue his campaign in the United States was thwarted by a short-lived armistice signed by Sir George Prevost, Governor-General of British North America, which gave the Americans time to regroup. Brock was killed by a sniper at the Battle of Queenston Heights. His last words were, 'Push on, don't mind me.'

Pax Britannica

Trafalgar veteran, Vice-Admiral Sir Edward Codrington was not supposed to sink the fleets of Turkey and Egypt. He was supposed to be on a diplomatic mission to enforce a ceasefire during the Greek War of Independence.

When Greece sought to throw off the rule of the Ottomans in 1821, the British public were largely sympathetic. The poet Lord Byron rode to the rescue, along with Sir Thomas Cochrane, naval officer, disgraced MP and a mercenary in the South America wars of independence.

France was also sympathetic, as was Russia. However, the danger was that, if the Ottomans were substantially weakened by a defeat, Russia would take Constantinople and the gates to the Black Sea. Meanwhile, the Sultan had called for help to his vassal Mehemet Ali, the Ottoman viceroy of Egypt. Ali sent the Egyptian army and navy under the command of his son, Ibrahim Pasha.

In 1827, Britain, France and Russia signed the Treaty

of London, agreeing to enforce an armistice in the Greco-Turkish conflict. The Greeks agreed to the ceasefire and Codrington was sent on board the eight-four gun *Asia* to prevent the Turco-Egyptian fleet from intervening. He arrived outside the port of Navarino on the Peloponnesus with a squadron of British, French and Russian ships. Even so, they were outnumbered and outgunned by Ibrahim Pasha's force inside.

Just then, news came that Cochrane had attacked Patras, breaking the ceasefire, and Ibrahim asked for permission to retaliate. But Codrington refused to let him sail, saying he had come to uphold the armistice, not see it broken further. Ibrahim would not take no for an answer. The next day, his fleet tried to sail out of the harbour to fight Cochrane. But Codrington intercepted the fleet and forced it back into the bay.

Having failed to break out, Ibrahim Pasha disembarked some of his troops, who set about raping and pillaging the surrounding area. Codrington was not going to put up with this and sailed into harbour to restore order. Ibrahim was ready for him. His fleet was drawn up in a semicircle, which would expose the incomers to fire from the entire fleet. He sent a messenger on a small boat, saying Codrington had not asked permission to enter the harbour and demanded that he withdraw. Codrington replied that he had come to *give* orders, not to take them.

The frigate *Dartmouth* launched a boat to tell a nearby Turkish ship to pull back. The Turks assumed it was carrying a boarding party and opened fire. Soon the bay was a blaze of gunfire. When the smoke cleared, sixty Turkish and Egyptians ships were sunk or burned, and there were six thousand dead and another four thou himself himself sand wounded. The Allies had 181 dead and 480 wound. Not a single ship was lost.

Codrington was seen as a hero by the British public for a second time. He was bedecked with medals from Britain, France, Russia and Greece. Meanwhile, the government fumed and the British, French and Russian ambassadors made grovelling apologies to the Sultan.

Ibrahim Pasha went on to defeat the Ottoman army in Syria and Mehmet Ali became the hereditary ruler of a Egypt, though he was, in fact, an Albanian.

Freedom of the press

These days it is possible to prevent vital information being leaked to the enemy by censoring the press, or embedding journalists with the military to stop them wandering off on their own and discovering things they shouldn't. Things were different in the days of William Howard Russell, now thought of as the first modern war correspondent, who wrote for *The Times* during the Crimean War.

On 23 October 1854, *The Times* carried one of his articles that gave the exact dispositions of the regiments and a powder store outside Sevastopol. They immediately came under bombardment. It was clear to Lord Raglan that the Russians had got their information from *The Times*, which arrived in Sevastopol before it reached the British camp at Balaclava. Raglan wrote complaining:

The paid agent of the Emperor of Russia could not serve his master better than does the correspondent of the paper that has the largest circulation in Europe . . . I am very doubtful whether a British army can long be maintained in the presence of such a powerful enemy, that enemy having at his command through the English press and from London to his headquarters by telegraph, every detail that can be required of the numbers, condition and equipment of his opponent's force.

But nothing was done to censor Russell's reports. As the tsar said, 'We have no need of spies: we have *The Times*.'

Mad in Madagascar

In 1883, the French tried to invade Madagascar. Defending the island were three Englishmen – the British Consul Mr Pakenham, the commander of the Royal Navy sloop *Dryad* Captain Johnstone and a British missionary named Shaw.

A powerful French naval squadron under Rear Admiral Pierre turned up off the capital Tamatave and threatened to bombard it. Pakenham protested and was told to mind his own business. So he got Johnstone to send twenty sailors from the *Dryad* to defend the consulate. Pierre interpreted this as an invasion of the island by the British and six large French warships promptly began firing.

There were no government troops in Tamatave at the time. The fort was empty and did not even fly the Madagascan flag, and the bombardment only succeeded in setting fire to the natives' huts, which were made of straw and leaves. The fire threatened to engulf the many French houses in Tamatave as well, until it was extinguished by rain. The following morning six hundred French troops were sent ashore. Pierre declared martial law. Again Pakenham protested, asking who the enemy was.

A French picket was sent to guard the home of a missionary named Shaw, which had been damaged by French shelling. Drugs were taken from his dispensary and bottles of wine had been taken from his cellar. When Shaw went to Pierre to protest, he was arrested and charged with attempting to poison French soldiers with drugged wine. Pierre then insisted that Pakenham leave Tamatave within twenty-four hours. But Pakenham was suffering from a kidney complaint and died after only twelve. Johnstone then appointed himself consul.

Pierre sent men to stop and search the British steamer *Taymouth Castle* – an act of piracy – and demanded Johnstone hand over correspondence between the *Dryad* and the Admiralty – an act of war. Johnstone resisted and put his tiny sloop at action stations, ready to take on the might of the French fleet.

Fortunately, it did not come to that. The British consul at Zanzibar got to hear of the situation. The Royal Navy sent a squadron. It was decided that Admiral Pierre was going mad and he was recalled. Shaw was released after fifty-four days and given £1,000 in compensation.

Two years later, France and Madagascar signed a treaty, whose terms were disputed. In 1896, France finally annexed the island, but only after six thousand French troops had died of malaria on a second expedition.

Fishing expedition

In 1914, Field Marshal John French, head of the British Expeditionary Force, and General Charles Lanrezac, commanding the French Fifth Army, had a low opinion of one another. Lanrezac considered French an idiot, while French thought Lanrezac no gentleman. Neither spoke the other's language and they refused to use an interpreter for the sake of security. This caused endless misunderstandings. On one occasion, French pointed at a map of the River Meuse and asked whether the Germans would cross it by the bridge at Huy. Indeed, it was the only bridge they could use and they were crossing it at the time. French's French was so excruciating, Lanrezac had to turn to an aide to discover what he was saying. When Lanrezac finally understood French's query, he said to the aide, 'Tell the Marshal, I think the Germans have come to the Meuse to fish.' The French commander-in-chief, Marshal Joseph Joffre, eventually had to remove Lanrezac in the interests of the Anglo-French alliance.

103

CHAPTER FOUR

Underestimating the Enemy

HE ASSUMED SUPERIORITY OF THE Englishman often leads him to underestimate any enemy. However, the English, with their penchant for amateurism, are also often underestimated by those more militarily minded who are set against them.

1066 and all that

Following the death of Edward the Confessor in 1066, England was ripe for invasion by competing claimants to the throne. One of them was the king of Norway, Harald Hardrada – or 'Hard-rule' – also known as Harald the Ruthless. He was a professional soldier who had fought in Scandinavia, in Russia under the grand prince of Kiev Yaroslav the Wise, and in Bulgaria and Sicily as part of the elite Varangian Guard of the Byzantine emperor Michael IV. In September 1066, he landed in northern England with fifteen thousand men on board three hundred longships, easily overcoming the defenders at the Battle of Fulford.

Harald then assumed that the English incumbent Harold Godwinson would recognise his claim to the throne and proceeded inland with only half his forces. It was an unseasonably hot summer and when his army reached Stamford Bridge they stripped off their armour and went for a swim in the River Derwent. They put no pickets out and, when they saw the glint of sunlight reflected from metal and the dust kicked up by Harold's army making a forced march from London, they assumed it was a fresh contingent of Vikings approaching from the coast.

The English outnumbered Harald's men. They were heavily armed, while the Norwegians had no time to don

their armour and grab their weapons. One Viking berserker managed to hold the bridge single-handed for some time. When he was overcome, the battle was lost. Hardrada was killed and only twenty-four of the three hundred longships were needed to transport the survivors home.

Harold's men had plenty to celebrate and, when they turned up outside Hastings to meet the invasion forces of William of Normandy three weeks later, it was noticed that they were drunk, even though the battle began first thing in the morning.

Awake the Wake!

After William the Conqueror's victory at the Battle of Hastings in 1066, the Normans began slowly to colonise England. However, there was considerable resistance. In 1070, Sweyn II of Denmark (1047–74) arrived at the mouth of the Humber and was expected to make a bid for the crown. He sent soldiers to secure the Isle of Ely as a base for an invasion. Then it could be reached by sea-going vessels from the Wash and River Ouse, while being protected to the landward side by swamps and waterways. The Danes were joined by local people, many of whom were of Danish extraction. A band of Danish sailors seized the opportunity to sack Peterborough Abbey to keep its treasures out of the hands of the newly appointed Norman abbot and took refuge on Ely. Soon after, Sweyn made peace with William and the Danes returned home. Ely then became home to Anglo-Saxon fugitives, including the earl of Northumbria.

In 1071, William besieged the isle. One of the defenders was Hereward the Wake. It is thought that the cognomen 'the Wake' – thought to signify 'the wakeful one' – was added later, appearing first in the fourteenth century. However, it may derive from his relationship with the manor of Bourne in Lincolnshire, which, from the mid-twelfth century, belonged to the Wake family.

Hereward the Wake was celebrated in ballads, which, no doubt, exaggerated his exploits. During the first quarter of the twelfth century, a monk in Ely Abbey wrote the *Gesta Herewardi*. The author claimed that he drew on first-hand accounts. Though by then Hereward was probably dead, a number of his comrades-in-arms would have still been alive and, though elderly, capable of recalling their old campaigns. And from the *Gesta* it seems certain that Hereward was a formidable foe whom the Conqueror repeatedly underestimated.

According to the *Gesta*, Hereward had been outlawed at the age of eighteen and was in exile when William invaded. He returned to find that his family were dead and his estates had been taken by the French. Having donned his chain mail, he killed fourteen of them and took back his property. Hereward quickly became leader of a growing army of fugitives, the condemned and disinherited, while William had subjugated the rest of the country.

Hereward learnt that Frederick, the brother of the old Earl William de Warenne, was boasting that he would personally take Hereward into the king's presence for punishment or cut off his head and set it up at a crossroads, while driving all Hereward's followers into exile. But Hereward then learnt that Frederick had arrived in Norfolk with a military force. One evening while Frederick was plotting the death of Hereward, the outlaw arrived and killed him.

The rebels on the Isle of Ely invited Hereward to join them. However, the Earl de Warenne, whose brother Hereward had slain, was preparing ambushes along the roads that led out to the Isle through the swamp. Hereward skirted the ambushes and reached safety across the river in Ely. The earl urged his men to swim the river to avenge his brother. They said that this was impossible. All the earl could do was shout across the river, 'Oh, would that your master, that limb of Satan, were in my grasp now; he should truly taste punishment and death!'

Hereward replied, 'But if by good luck we two happened to be by ourselves anywhere, you wouldn't be so keen to have me in your feeble grasp nor be glad that we met!'

Then Hereward fired an arrow with such force, that, although it rebounded from the earl's mail coat, it knocked him from his horse, rendering him unconscious.

When the king heard about this he grew angry and decided to take Ely by force. He moved his whole army to Aldreth, where the water surrounding the Isle was narrower. They brought timber and stone and began building a causeway out through the swamp. At the river, they joined large tree trunks together with beams, supported underneath by inflated sheepskins. However, greedy for plunder, the whole army rushed onto the bridge all at once, the roadway sank and the soldiers drowned.

The monk writing the *Gesta* remarked, 'To this day many of them are dragged out of the depths of those waters in rotting armour. I've sometimes seen this myself.'

Only one man out of the entire company reached the Isle. After being shown the island's defences, he was allowed to go so he could tell the king that Ely boasted a strongly fortified location occupied by courageous soldiers. The Earl de Warenne grew angry, saying that he had been deceived by Hereward. But the man insisted that he was only reporting what he had seen with his own eyes.

A knight named Ivo de Taillebois spoke up. 'For a long time now I've known a certain old woman who could by her art alone, if she were present, crush all their courage and defence and drive them all out of the island in terror,' he said.

The king ordered the hag to be brought to him secretly. In the meantime, he took his entire army to Aldreth once again and ordered all the fishermen in the area to bring their boats to ferry the materials needed to build fortifications. Hereward disguised himself as a fisherman. All day they ferried timber across the river. That night, when they had finished work, Hereward set fire to the timber. The fortifications were burned and several men were killed.

After that the Normans then guarded the site at Aldreth more closely. It took a week to complete one earthwork and set up four wooden bastions to carry the siege engines. Meanwhile, Hereward had built ramparts on the Isle opposite them. Then the French army began their attack with de Taillebois's witch in a raised position in their midst. Protected from all sides, she chanted and cast spells. She bared her arse at the rebels – three times. Hereward's men had made their way out through the swamps and set fire to reeds and brambles. The wind blew the smoke and flames towards the king's men, who fled for their lives. Many lost their way and disappeared into the swamp. Others were cut down by arrows. Knights found that their lances were useless against these guerrilla attacks. Even the king arrived back at camp with an arrow sticking from his shield. In the tumult, the witch was toppled from her elevated position, fell to the ground and broke her neck.

As the king had failed to take the Isle by force, he decreed that all the surrounding lands owned by the churchmen of Ely should be divided among his royal guard. So the Abbot of Ely decided to make peace behind Hereward's back, provided the king return the church land. William occupied the island and Hereward and his men were forced to flee. They eluded their pursuers for a while by putting the shoes on their horses back-to-front. But as the King's men eventually caught up with them, it was clear that they were going to have to fight.

Hereward positioned his archers and slingsmen in the branches of the trees. Despite being vastly outnumbered, Hereward and his horsemen made repeated forays on the enemy lines. After doing as much damage as possible they galloped back to the safety of the greenwood, where the Normans dared not follow them because of the men in the branches above.

According to the *Gesta*, Hereward took on and killed several of the king's champions. There was even one who hid in a lavatory and put his head up through the hole in the seat to beg for mercy. In this case, Hereward spared him. Eventually, the *Gesta* says, King William pardoned him and Hereward lived on for many years as a loyal subject.

Many of the tales told about Hereward the Wake are similar to those told later about Robin Hood, and it is thought that the early English freedom fighter may have been one of the models on which the English outlaw was based.

111

Stupidity at Stirling Bridge

William de Warenne's descendant John de Warenne, seventh Earl of Surrey, was no Brave Heart. When, at sixty-five, he was appointed Warden of Scotland in August 1296, he paid a quick visit and returned to England, saying the Scottish climate did not suit his health. However, when de Warenne's son-in-law, Scotland's King John Balliol, refused to supply troops for Edward I's war against France and even signed a treaty with the French, de Warenne had no choice but to return, winning an easy victory at the Battle of Dunbar. Balliol was deposed. Edward I claimed sovereignty over Scotland and removed the Stone of Scone, Scotland's traditional coronation stone, taking it to Westminster Abbey, where it remained for seven hundred years.

The following spring saw the rebellion of Sir William Wallace. Once more, de Warenne was sent to sort things out. But Edward had spent so much on his wars against the French, Scots and Welsh that he was short of money and de Warenne was accompanied by the portly Hugh de Cressingham, England's overweight Treasurer. He was there to see that none of the king's money was wasted and, as de Warenne had achieved such an easy victory at Dunbar, he sent a division under Henry Percival back to Northumbria to save their wages.

Wallace hid his army in the wooded hills overlooking the fast-flowing River Forth at Stirling. The wooden bridge there was only wide enough for two horsemen abreast. Sir Richard Lundy, a Scots knight who had recently come over to the English, said that he knew of a ford nearby where men could cross thirty abreast. But Cressingham said, 'There is no use, sir, in drawing out this business any longer and wasting the king's revenues for nothing.'

The following morning, the English began crossing the bridge, only to be recalled because de Warenne had overslept. When they crossed again, Wallace waited until about a third of the English army was assembled on the marshy ground to the north of the river. Then the Scottish charged down the slope armed with spears and axes. They quickly blocked off the bridgehead so that no more English could cross and those who had crossed could not retreat. All those on the north bank were slaughtered, including the corpulent Cressingham.

De Warenne still had most of his army intact, including a formidable contingent of archers. But he had lost heart. He ordered the bridge to be destroyed and retreated to England, while his Scots allies rallied to Wallace and attacked his fleeing soldiers.

Cressingham's body was stripped and flayed. It is said that Wallace used a strip of his skin as a baldric, or sword belt.

Bugger-up at Burgos

Even the Duke of Wellington could have an off day. After defeating 'forty thousand Frenchmen in forty minutes' at Salamanca in July 1812 and taking Madrid in August, he laid siege to Burgos in September. He had just eight cannons with him, leaving a hundred siege guns at Madrid, dismissing Burgos as just another hill fort, like those he had been used to taking in India. But it wasn't. It was an impregnable modern fort built on the solid foundations of a medieval castle.

Admiral Sir Home Popham offered to send heavy cannons from the fleet, but Wellington declined, believing it would take too much time. He sent five infantry divisions to assault Burgos. But with no breach in the wall this was pointless. When red-hot shot failed to set the French stores alight, the answering barrage destroyed the British guns. Then it began to rain, extinguishing all hope of a blaze. The French even had the temerity to launch a sally out of the fort, occupy British trenches and drink their grog.

By that time the English had lost two thousand men – against French casualties of just three hundred – and Wellington was forced to withdraw. During their retreat, his men got drunk on local wine. The French captured three thousand stragglers and two divisions got lost. When Wellington was told by the officer in charge of the support column that he had lost his baggage train, he replied, 'I can't be surprised, for I cannot find my army.'

Lucked out at Lucknow

Another commander who should not have listened to his financial adviser was Sir Henry Lawrence, chief commissioner in Lucknow during the Indian Mutiny. Lucknow was not affected by the Mutiny – at first. However, Lawrence's revenue commissioner, Martin Gubbins, urged him to take what troops he had out of Lucknow and attack five hundred mutineers who had assembled at Chinhat, eight miles away. They had only one gun, Gubbins said. Then Gubbins received a second report saying that there were, in fact, six thousand mutineers at Chinhat with numerous guns, but he neglected to update Lawrence, believing that, with one show of strength by the redcoats, the mutineers would run away. Besides, if the British did not attack, Gubbins said, they would be 'branded as cowards at the bar of history'.

Lawrence assembled a force of 220 Indian infantry, eight Sikh cavalry, eleven guns and three hundred men of the 32nd (Cornwall) Regiment of Foot. They had had no breakfast and were suffering the after effects of a night of heavy drinking. There had been no time to clean their rifles. Even so, delays meant that they missed out leaving in the cool of the morning. Instead they set out on their eight-mile march, hung over, in the heat of the day.

Arriving at Chindit, Lawrence found his men outnumbered ten to one. Instead of marching back to Lucknow, he asked Colonel Case, commanding the 32nd, if his men were fit for battle. Before Case could answer, the regiment's previous commander, Colonel Inglis, now Lawrence's second-in-command, said that they were.

They advanced, only to be fired on by mutineers hidden in the trees. Meanwhile, their own rifles misfired. The Indian gunners and the Sikh cavalry promptly deserted. The mutineers then manoeuvred and tried to cut the British off from Lucknow. Lawrence had no choice but to retreat. The retreat turned into a rout. Lawrence then resorted to a desperate bluff. He turned the artillery pieces on the enemy and, although he had no ammunition or powder, he stationed a man next to each holding a lighted brand. This was enough to halt the sepoy cavalry, allowing the survivors to reach Lucknow – though some died of heatstroke within sight of the residency. Of the original 600, 293 were killed and 78 wounded.

The Siege of Lucknow then began. On the first day of the siege, an eight-inch shell hit Lawrence's bedroom in the residency. Two days later, it was hit again – this time

with Lawrence in it. The siege lasted for 148 days. The largest number of Victoria Crosses awarded in a single day – twenty-four – were earned at Lucknow on 16 November 1857 during the relief of the city.

Zulu time

The British like to celebrate their victory at Rorke's Drift on 22 January 1879, when 120 redcoats held off four or five thousand Zulus with minimal losses. But that same day they had suffered an overwhelming defeat at the hands of the Zulu just seven miles away at Isandhlwana.

On 11 January, the British column under Lord Chelmsford had crossed the Buffalo River into Zululand at Rorke's Drift and encamped below a rocky hill known to the Zulus as Isandhlwana, leaving men behind to guard the ford. Chelmsford then set out with roughly 2,500 men to search for the Zulu army, leaving a mixed force of 950 Europeans and 850 natives under the command of Lieutenant-Colonel Henry Pulleine behind at the camp. They did not follow standing orders and entrench, nor did they even circle the wagons into some sort of defensive laager. The infantry were armed with the latest breach-loading Martini–Henry rifles and they had two field guns, while the enemy were armed only with spears and cowhide shields. What could go wrong?

At 11 a.m., a force of 20,000–25,000 Zulu approached and formed up into the classic buffalo's-horn formation. British morale was high as disciplined volleys of rifle fire thinned the encircling Zulus. When one of Lord Chelmsford's staff officers, Lieutenant-Colonel Henry Crealock, heard the news, he said, 'Actually attacking our camp! Most amusing!' But soon the ammunition began to dwindle and rifles began to jam in the heat. The forty to fifty rounds they had been issued with were soon exhausted, but there were plenty of reserves on the wagons. However, they were in heavy wooden boxes, enclosed with copper bands, each held down with nine screws. Some of the screws had rusted in place and were hard to shift.

There was also a shortage of screwdrivers and, according to regulations, only one box could be opened at a time. Every round had to be accounted for and the quartermaster of the 24th Foot refused to give ammunition to the Natal Native Horse, who had to go foraging for bullets elsewhere. Lieutenant Horace Smith-Dorrien took matters into his own hands and began smashing the crates open with an axe. He shovelled cartridges into men's helmets – only to be told to stop as he had not got the right requisition papers.

With no ammunition in their rifles, but plenty still safely in its boxes, the British were overwhelmed. By 4 p.m., it was all over. Every living thing in the camp – including the horses, dogs and mules – had been killed. The world was shocked that a modern European army equipped with the latest rifles and artillery could be defeated, let alone massacred, by spear-wielding tribesmen.

The British, of course, did not leave it at that and began to take the Zulu seriously. At the Battle of Kambula two months later, they decisively beat them, putting an end to the independence of Zululand. The fighting at Rorke's Drift was merely a sideshow. If the garrison there had been lost, there is no indication that the Zulu would have invaded Natal.

Smith-Dorrien was one of the few who managed to escape the massacre. He went on to fight in the First World War, where, disregarding Sir John French's order to retreat, his men stopped a huge German force at Le Cateau, allowing the British Expeditionary Force to disengage in good order. He was, naturally, dismissed.

The invasion of Iraq, First World War style

In November 1914, the British invaded Mesopotamia, seizing the oil refineries around the port of Basra. Resistance was minimal, so Lieutenant-General Arthur Barrett set off up the Tigris River with the Sixth Indian Division, capturing the town of Kurna 120 miles from the sea. He was then replaced with the arrogant, ambitious Major-General Charles Townshend. Under orders from General Sir John Nixon, Townshend pushed on up the Tigris. Although this exceeded their authority, they thought that, if they could take Baghdad, it would relieve the pressure on the British forces fighting in Gallipoli.

Townshend organised a fleet of barges known as 'Townshend's regatta' and took the town of Amara, a further ninety miles upriver. With their supply lines stretched to breaking point, Townshend took Kut. However, the Turks withdrew in good order and set up defensive positions at Ctesiphon, blocking the way to Baghdad. Hampered by the shallowness of the river, Townshend took the main Turkish position at Ctesiphon after heavy and costly fighting. But a counterattack the following day forced the British to retreat.

Townshend withdrew to Kut, where he was besieged. When attempts to relieve him failed, he tried to treat with the enemy. After a siege lasting 147 days, he eventually surrendered. His 13,000 men were led off on a death march into captivity; 70 per cent never returned. Meanwhile, Townshend was held in a luxurious villa on Prinkipo Island near Constantinople, where he dined and hunted with Turkish dignitaries. When he returned to Britain, he was knighted, though he thought he deserved a peerage. He had lost forty thousand men in all. He later became an MP. When he died in 1924, he was buried with full military honours.

The invasion of Iraq, Second World War style

In February 1941, Lieutenant Arthur Wellesley – the great great-great-great-great-grandson of the first Duke of Wellington – was in Palestine with the Household Cavalry when the order came to shoot their horses.

'I had to take fourteen elderly horses into the Judean hills and shoot them,' he said. 'Those lovely old black horses ended their days on a bleak Palestinian hill to become fodder for vultures and jackals.'

Instead, the Household Cavalry were issued with Morris trucks and told to invade Iraq. They were given little support, as the commander-in-chief in the Middle East, General Sir Archibald Wavell, was against the whole venture. He wanted to negotiate with Rashid Ali al-Gailani, a pro-German pan-Arabist who had just seized power in a military coup. Nevertheless, Winston Churchill ordered the attack.

The invasion force was dubbed Habforce, as its first task was to raise the siege on the RAF base at al-Habbaniya. It drove five hundred miles across the desert following the oil pipelines in temperatures up to 134°F in the shade.

'It was very disagreeable,' said the future eighth Duke of Wellington. 'It was so hot that you could not keep a man sitting there for more than half an hour. Obviously, if you've got to do a job like this it's better to do it in the cooler months.'

The convoy was attacked by a German fighter-bomber, but, once they arrived at al-Habbaniya, resistance crumbled.

'The Iraqis were held off by a very spirited defence by the RAF, so they couldn't enter,' said Wellesley. 'The moment we came within sight of them, they gave up.'

The next objective was Baghdad, where they found they were outgunned by the Iraqi defenders, who had two Vickers machine guns. After a British trooper was killed out on a reconnoitre, Wellesley and thirty men went out to try to find the machine-gun emplacements.

'If those infernal guns were still there I thought we would soon know,' he said. 'We walked twenty-five yards, fifty yards . . . when we had gone nearly a hundred yards I was beginning to think we had got away with it. It came as almost a surprise when a storm of machine-gun fire descended on us. We tried to wriggle into the sand and waited for the terrible cacophony to stop. Luckily, they'd opened fire just a shade too soon.'

They planned to call in an RAF airstrike, but then a twenty-five-pounder opened fire and the Iraqis surrendered. Rashid Ali fled. The whole invasion had taken just thirty days.

CHAPTER FIVE

Crazy Campaigns

HE GREAT MILITARY THEORIST Carl von
Clausewitz said famously, 'No campaign plan
survives the first contact with the enemy.' In
many campaigns in Old England, the plan
did not even survive *that* long.

The War of Jenkins' Ear

In 1738, Captain Robert Jenkins appeared before a
committee of the House of Commons with a specimen in a
jar. He said it was his severed ear, pickled for the purpose. It
had been cut off in the West Indies by Spanish coast guards,
who had boarded his ship, pillaged it and set it adrift. The
ear had been given back to him with the instruction to give
it to his king, George II.

Others maintain that he had lost the ear in the pillory
while he was being flogged for theft, or worse. Nevertheless,
the following year, Britain and Spain went to war over the
severed lug. When war was declared, the bells rang out in

123

England. Hearing them, Prime Minister Robert Walpole said, 'They may ring their bells now, they will be wringing their hands before long.'

The war began with Admiral Edward Vernon attacking the silver-exporting town of Porto Bello on the coast of Panama with six ships of the line. He seized the town in under twenty-four hours, destroyed its fortifications, the harbour and its warehouses. This victory was celebrated with a dinner in London, where 'Rule Britannia' was played for the first time. More medals were awarded for the attack on Porto Bello than any other event in the eighteenth century and Portobello Road in London was named in its honour.

Vernon was then sent to take Cartagena in Colombia. This was an altogether more formidable expedition with 29 ships of the line, 157 other warships and transports, and 11,000 soldiers and marines under the command of Major-General Thomas Wentworth. While Vernon was a daredevil on the high seas, Wentworth was a man more at home on the parade ground than the battlefield.

The rainy season in the Caribbean brought with it tropical diseases, so Vernon favoured a lightning attack before it started. But, when Wentworth was put ashore, he dug in, in preparation for the counterattack, as specified by the military manuals. This took two days. Meanwhile, Spaniards fortified the island of Tierra Bomba, which guarded the entrance to the harbour.

Vernon was infuriated by the delay and sent a letter telling Wentworth to get on with it. However, with the Spanish positions now fortified, he needed his engineering officer, Jonas Moore, who had not yet arrived. Meanwhile, the landing force was taking casualties. This was largely Wentworth's fault. He had set up his artillery in line with the camps, so, when the Spanish attacked the guns, cannon fire that overshot would land among the British tents. More than a hundred men were killed or wounded on the first day.

When Moore turned up, he surveyed the hastily constructed Fort San Luis and calculated that, to take it, he would need sixteen hundred men to build a siege battery. Wentworth asked Vernon for the return of a number of soldiers he had lent him to make up for shortages in naval manpower. Vernon refused, maintaining that there was no need for a siege battery to overcome such a feeble fort. Wentworth then said that he did not have the firepower to breach the walls. Vernon insisted that he did not need it. The Spanish would run away if the infantry attacked. He was right. Meanwhile, Moore set up his guns for a bombardment. The Spanish fired back and he was killed. But then, at the first sight of approaching redcoats, the Spanish abandoned the fort. By that time battle casualties had risen to 130, but Wentworth had lost 850 to disease.

The men were re-embarked and transported across the harbour to attack Fort San Lazar. Wentworth wanted to land five thousand men for the attack. Vernon insisted that all he would need were fifteen hundred. He was right. Realising that he was hopelessly outnumbered, the Spanish commander Don Blas de Lezo decided that the best he could hope for was to make a fighting withdrawal, delaying the British until the start of the rainy season, which would put an end to the campaign for two months.

When Wentworth was landed, instead of attacking the fort and the city, which were his for the taking, he set up camp several miles from the fort and prepared for a long siege. Again Vernon was infuriated.

'Delay is your worst enemy,' he wrote. 'We hope that you will be master of St Lazar tomorrow.'

But Wentworth insisted that the fort could not be taken by an assault. Its walls were too high. He asked for a naval bombardment. Vernon refused, saying he would not risk bringing his ships in so close to land. He then forced Wentworth's hand. No tools were sent ashore, so Wentworth could not waste time building siege batteries. And no tents were landed, so Wentworth's men would have to sleep in the open until they took the fort.

Wentworth had no choice but to plan a night assault on the fort. Colonel Wynyard would take the main force and attack the southern wall of the fort, while another column under Colonel Grant would attack the north side. Wynyard's column would be guided by Spanish deserters who assured him that there was no trench work to the south. However, in the darkness they got lost and found themselves scrambling up a steep hill to the east of the fort to discover it was protected by three lines of trenches.

Preparing for the assault, they called up the ladders needed to climb the walls, only to find that they were at the back of the column. By the time the message ordering them up reached the rear, the men carrying them had made off. The Spanish then opened fire. Wynyard had no alternative but to attack. But, instead of leading a ferocious charge, he marched his men up as if they were on the parade ground and had them fire a volley and reload as if it were a drill. They were cut down by Spanish rifle fire and grapeshot. Eventually, they had no alternative but to withdraw.

Grant's column did no better. The Spanish artillery cut through the neat British ranks. As the dawn came up, the cannons of Cartagena joined in the massacre. As Grant lay dying, he said, 'The general ought to hang the guides and the king ought to hang the general.'

Others blamed the admiral for not bombarding the fort.

Disease then ravaged the troops. Eyewitness John Pembroke said, 'By honest count we lost eighteen thousand men dead, and, according to a Spanish soldier we captured, they lost at most two hundred. Admiral One Leg with his excellent leadership and fire killed nine thousand of our men, General Fever killed a like number. When I last saw the harbour of Cartagena, its surface was grey with the rotting bodies of our men, who died so rapidly that we could not bury them.'

When the rains came, the British had to reboard their ships and sail away. Of the original 11,000 only 1,700 were fit for action. Fifty ships were sunk or abandoned due to a shortage of crew. However, a medal had already been struck to celebrate the victory, showing Don Blas de Lezo kneeling before Admiral Vernon. It had to be quietly withdrawn. Nevertheless, Vernon was commemorated by Lawrence

Washington, one of the colonial troops at Cartagena. He renamed his plantation in Virginia Mount Vernon in honour of the admiral. After Lawrence's death in 1752, his half-brother George inherited it.

The feud between Vernon and Wentworth continued. Next they attacked Santiago on the southern tip of Cuba. Vernon knew that a direct attack from the sea would be difficult and decided to land the army to the east – without telling Wentworth. As Wentworth's men made their way slowly across difficult terrain, Vernon sent dispatches back to London defaming him. He got his brother to publish accounts criticising Wentworth and even sent one of his captains back to London, where he wrote *An Account of the Expedition to Cartagena*, which was less than flattering to the army.

Vernon then failed in another attack on Panama, but he returned to England with his popularity undimmed. He became an MP, while Wentworth was sent off to Flanders to command a division during the War of the Austrian Succession.

Not-so-naughty Napoleon

You would have thought that Napoleon would have started the Napoleonic Wars. After all, they are named after him and he was a military dictator who, by all accounts, was hell-bent on the conquest of Europe, if not the world. But, when he took over as consul in 1799, the first thing he did was to write to George III, expressing his desire for peace – to the annoyance of the government of William Pitt the

Younger. The French Revolutionary Wars that had been going on for seven years suited the Tories, who wanted a clear victory over Jacobinism and the old enemy France. But Napoleon made overtures to the Russians. Then, after he had pushed the Austrians out of Germany and Italy, he made peace with them, leaving France secure behind the frontiers Julius Caesar had established for Gaul – the Rhine, the Alps and the Pyrenees. Even Britain signed the Treaty of Amiens in 1802 and peace broke out across Europe. France now went on to a peacetime footing. Meanwhile, Britain doubled the size of its army.

Under the Treaty of Amiens, Britain was supposed to leave the island of Malta and return it to the Knights Hospitallers. But the British refused to go. Napoleon was naturally suspicious of the British. They had occupied his home island of Corsica in 1794. Britain's excuse for not leaving Malta was that a new grand master of the Knights of Malta had not yet been named. Napoleon got the pope to appoint one. The British then claimed that Malta was not secure. Napoleon got the King of Naples to send two thousand troops to the island, but when they arrived the British would not allow them to man the forts. Napoleon even suggested the Russians send a peacekeeping force to the island. Britain responded by calling up the militia and recruiting ten thousand more sailors.

The reason for Britain's belligerence was that William Pitt and the Tories hated France and saw Napoleon as the devil incarnate. They wanted to hold onto Malta as a naval base in the Mediterranean. The British had signed the Treaty of Amiens, though.

'You must respect treaties,' Napoleon insisted to the British ambassador. 'Woe to those who do not respect treaties. They shall answer for it to all Europe.'

But Britain still refused to leave Malta and, on 18 May 1803, declared war on France once more.

The following year, the French uncovered a British-backed plot to assassinate Bonaparte. His chief of police, Joseph Fouché, suggested that the best way to discourage any further conspiracy was for Napoleon to make himself emperor. That way he would have an hereditary heir, so an assassin would have less to gain. Only the head of state would change, not the regime.

The one way Napoleon could strike back against the British was to cross the Channel and invade. Any chance of doing that was scotched by the annihilation of the French and Spanish fleets at the Battle of Trafalgar in 1805. Britain also succeeded in building a new anti-French coalition.

Another way Napoleon could defend himself against the British was to attack British India, overland, through Afghanistan. But in 1807, he signed the Treaty of Tilsit with Tsar Alexander, who promised to attack the British, overland, in India. But Alexander openly ignored the treaty and continued trading with the British while secretly sounding out the Austrians and Prussians in the hope of building a new anti-French alliance. This led to Napoleon's disastrous invasion of Russia in 1812.

Even after his defeat in Russia, Napoleon was not a spent force. A new coalition formed against him. At a peace conference in Prague in 1813, Austria offered favourable peace terms, but before Napoleon replied Austria declared war once again. By this time, France was exhausted and, when allied armies took Paris, Napoleon abdicated and was exiled to Elba. This was supposed to be his own little fiefdom, but his ex-wife Josephine, whom he still loved, was not allowed to accompany him. Napoleon's current wife, Marie-Louise of Austria, and their son were also prevented from joining him by her father, the Emperor of Austria. She soon had a new lover and probably would not have wanted to visit him on Elba, anyway.

Under the Treaty of Fontainebleau, which governed Napoleon's exile, the French government was supposed to pay him an annual income of two million francs. They did not pay up and even threatened to confiscate his family's property. Threatened with being reduced to penury, Napoleon had little choice but to escape. When he returned to France in 1815, his troops rallied to his side. When he took power, he offered to make peace again, but the allies would have none of it. After a hundred days, he was narrowly defeated at the Battle of Waterloo and was sent into exile in St Helena, where he struggled to learn English.

None of this is to say that Napoleon would not have taken on the rest of Europe anyway. Maybe he would have. But he did not start the wars that bear his name. Others did, either by declaring war on France or by failing to fulfil their obligations under treaties they had signed. That is not to say that Napoleon was a good and honourable man. He abandoned two armies – one in Egypt, one in Russia. His military adventures cost the lives of at least half a million young Frenchmen, around one-sixth of the population of France, and affected the birthrate for decades to come.

The Battle of the River Plate – no, not that one

The British had few holdings in South America. But Commodore Home Popham liked the sound of the River Plate, or Río de la Plata – which is Spanish for 'River of Silver'. It may not be El Dorado, the legendary City of Gold, but it would do. Then, the province of Río de la Plata encompassed modern-day Argentina, Uruguay, Paraguay and Bolivia. It was the size of Western Europe. So in 1806 Popham 'borrowed' fourteen hundred men from the Cape of Good Hope garrison and set off to conquer it.

He had little reason to think he could succeed. A drunken American sea captain had told him that the colonists there were eager to throw off Spanish rule and would welcome the British as liberators. And an English ship's carpenter told him that Montevideo, which guarded the mouth of the estuary, was poorly defended.

Buoyed by this scant intelligence, Popham sailed directly to Buenos Aires, the largest city in South America with a population of seventy thousand. When the fleet was sighted, the Spanish Viceroy fled and the British took the city unopposed. One Spanish lady learnt of the invasion only when she found a British officer asleep on her sofa.

Popham sent the captured Spanish treasury back to London, where it was paraded through the streets. However, the inhabitants of Buenos Aires soon realised how weak the invasion force was. Gauchos and Creole irregulars took over the rest of the province, while Catholic priests stirred up the people in the city. Then a force of regular troops under

Captain Santiago Liniers marched in and took the English invaders captive, while Popham looked on from his ships.

But all was not lost. The British public had seen Popham's treasure being paraded through the streets and liked what they saw. So, unaware that Buenos Aires had been recaptured, the government had no alternative but to send another four thousand men under the command of Brigadier-General Samuel Auchmuty, an American loyalist who had been on the losing side in the War of Independence. Then the minister of war came up with an elaborate plan to send another four thousand men under Colonel Robert 'Black Bob' Craufurd to attack Chile. He was then approaching Buenos Aires from the west – presumably scaling the Andes on the way. No one knew quite how long this nine-hundred-mile journey would take, especially as the plan called for them to build a series of forts on the way. Meanwhile, the prime minister came up with a harebrained scheme to invade Mexico with simultaneous landings from east and west.

When Auchmuty arrived, he found Buenos Aires in Spanish hands. Instead, he turned his attention to Montevideo. Far from being ill-defended as Popham had been told, the city had more than a hundred artillery pieces behind stout walls. Nevertheless, despite being heavily outnumbered, Auchmuty's men took Montevideo.

The British government then sent General John Whitelocke to be the governor of Río de la Plata when it was subdued. Although he had been promoted rapidly through the ranks, Whitelocke had no experience of command. By then the Chile and Mexico expeditions had been cancelled and with him he brought the impetuous Craufurd and Major-General John Leveson Gower, another officer who had no combat experience. However, Gower was one of the family of the Marquesses of Stafford. Whitelocke deferred to him and, during the voyage, Gower devised an elaborate plan to recapture Buenos Aires.

Preparing for the assault in June 1807, Lord Muskerry, who knew the area better than anyone else in the British forces, pointed out that making a landing in the winter was madness. The hectoring and foul-mouthed Whitelocke took offence. The landings would go ahead, but Muskerry and his men – the best soldiers under Whitelocke's command – were left behind to garrison Montevideo.

While previously the landing had been made eight miles from Buenos Aires, the new landings took place thirty-two miles from the city – in a swamp. The guns got stuck and the supplies were ruined by seawater. Whitelocke then divided his 8,500 men into three forces, who soon lost touch with each other. The march on Buenos Aires took five days, exhausting the men's scant provisions.

Craufurd got there first and drove off the defending force. But, instead of letting him storm on into the city, Whitelocke called a halt, then revealed Gower's plan. Buenos Aires was built on a gridiron of narrow streets, where each block was a solidly built mini-fortress. Under Gower's plan, the men were to be divided into thirteen groups, advancing along parallel streets. There would to be no preliminary bombardment from sea or land. The city was to be taken at bayonet point and the men were ordered to unload their muskets and take the flints out. There was no time to delay, as the winter rains could begin any minute.

The Spaniards had brought cannons into the city, which could fire down the streets into the oncoming infantry. Others hid in the houses. After the British marched by, they emerged to fire on columns from the rear, while civilians rained down anything they could lay hands on from the flat roofs of the houses.

Craufurd had to take refuge in the church of San Domingo. Others found themselves trapped or beleaguered. Meanwhile, Whitelocke was completely unaware of the plight of his men. He remained in his headquarters outside the city, awaiting a message from the Spanish commander offering his surrender. But, when the message came the next day, it demanded *his* surrender. He sent his ADC, Captain Whittingham, to assess the situation. From the top of a building he could see regimental colours dotted around the city. But they were in isolated pockets. The British had suffered 1,200 casualties and the Spanish held 1,800 prisoners. The remaining 5,500 men were still fighting and could have taken the city, eventually. But, by then, they had lost all faith in Whitelocke. Craufurd was so angered by the fiasco that he had ordered his men to shoot Whitelocke if they saw him. Eventually, he had to surrender, while his men scrawled graffiti on the walls saying that Whitelocke was either a coward or a traitor, or both.

A belated bombardment was discounted, as it was liable to injure the British prisoners. The shallows around Buenos Aires made it impossible to bring in supplies and ammunition for the beleaguered troops, so Whitelocke had no alternative but to give up. He agreed to withdraw his forces from Río de la Plata in exchange for the return of British prisoners and supplies for the voyage home.

Whitelocke was court-martialled and cashiered, largely for the loss of Montevideo. Popham was court-martialled for leaving his station at the Cape of Good Hope without permission. He was admonished, but remained in the navy and went on to become a rear admiral. Auchmuty was given the thanks of Parliament. He went on to become a general and was knighted.

The Walcheren Campaign

There can scarcely have been a more futile military campaign than the invasion of the Dutch island of Walcheren in 1809. The aim was to attack the French invasion fleet in Flushing and relieve the Austrians who were fighting Napoleon in Germany. However, by the time the British force landed, the French fleet had been moved to Antwerp, which was fortified, and the Austrians had been beaten at the Battle of Wagram and were suing for peace.

As well as being futile, the campaign was doomed from the outset. Low-lying and swampy, Walcheren was known to be a breeding ground of disease. A French force that had landed there a few years before had suffered 80 per cent casualties.

In July 1809 the largest British expeditionary force ever assembled weighed anchor off the Kent coast. There were 35 ships of the line, another 292 warships of assorted sizes and 352 carrying 44,000 troops – more than were under Wellington's command in Portugal at the time. However, their commander, the elderly Earl of Chatham, has been passed over for command when Wellington was appointed but, since he was the older brother of the prime minister, William Pitt, it was thought fitting that he be given a consolation prize.

The fleet was commanded by Sir Richard Strachan. He had proved himself a bold seaman, but was known as 'Mad Dick' among his men for his ungovernable temper and intemperate language. His humour was not improved when their departure was delayed by bad weather. There was a shortage of pilots who knew the narrow channels around Walcheren, and Strachan had little experience of landing such a large army.

Lord Chatham was known as 'the late earl' for his difficulty of rising from his bed in the morning. On Walcheren he proved himself characteristically slothful. Although his men took Middleburg and Flushing, he missed an early opportunity to seize Antwerp. Instead they dug in on swampy Walcheren as the French moved into position on the other side of the River Scheldt.

There had been flooding on the island the previous year and the standing water left behind made the perfect breeding ground for mosquitoes. It was hot and steamy that summer and soon men were coming down with malaria. By the beginning of September there were more than eight thousand cases. The supply of quinine they had brought with them soon ran out and the few doctors they had also succumbed. Men were left to lie on the beaches in their own filth.

As sick men began to be returned home, the hospitals were overwhelmed with what they called Walcheren fever. This is now thought to be a lethal combination of malaria, typhus, typhoid and dysentery. Of the 12,000 troops who remained on Walcheren, by October, only 5,616 were fit for duty.

On 9 December, the last British troops were withdrawn from Walcheren. The adventure had cost £10 million and 4,066 dead, though only 106 officers and men had actually been killed in action. The rest had died, predictably, of disease. Some 12,000 of the survivors were so badly affected by fever that they would never serve again. By 1 February 1810, 11,513 were still carried on the sick list. Some had been transferred to Portugal, doubling the sick rolls there, and Wellington wrote, requesting that no further units from the Walcheren Campaign be sent to him.

Back in London, Chatham and Strachan blamed the failure of their mission on each other's lethargy and delays, leading to the epigram:

> Great Chatham, with his sabre drawn,
> Stood waiting for Sir Richard Strachan,
> Sir Richard, longing to be at 'em,
> Stood waiting for the Earl of Chatham.

Both were promoted. Both died in their beds of old age.

Admiral Lord Loincloth

With the outbreak of the First World War, Lake Tanganyika became the front line with German East Africa to the east, the Belgian Congo to the west and Britain's Northern Rhodesia to the south. But, in 1914, it was very much in German hands with two German gunboats – the forty-five-ton *Kingani* and the sixty-ton *Hedwig von Wissmann* – plying its waters. However, a big-game hunter named John Lee came up with the idea of transporting an armed motorboat over two thousand miles overland from Cape Town to challenge them. The Admiralty liked the idea so much they sent two – which were peremptorily requisitioned from the Greek Air Force.

Lee was made a lieutenant-commander in the Royal Naval Volunteer Reserve. However, the Admiralty insisted on having a regular naval officer in charge of the expedition. With the navy on wartime duty on the high seas, they could not spare anyone who was any good. However, there was a chap named Geoffrey Spicer-Simson who, though a lieutenant-commander, was currently a glorified filing clerk in

Naval Intelligence in the basement of Admiralty House. He had had a rather chequered career. As captain of a destroyer, he had collided with another vessel and been stripped of his command and posted ashore to dockside security. Later he was given command of a contraband control vessel, but after two weeks his gunboat was torpedoed in broad daylight while he was ashore in a hotel with a woman. Nevertheless, he would go on to command what he himself described as a 'harebrained' enterprise.

Spicer-Simson was something of an eccentric. When asked to name the two forty-foot motor launches, he called them *Dog* and *Cat*. By and large, the Royal Navy prefer more belligerent names for their vessels – *Victory*, *Conqueror*, *Repulse*. So they asked him to try again. He came up with *Mimi* and *Toutou*.

When the expedition arrived at Cape Town, Lee had gone ahead to reconnoitre the route. Spicer-Simson feared being outshone by Lee, the adventurer, and sent Sub-Lieutenant Douglas Hope to check up on him. Hope promptly reported that Lee had got drunk and insulted the Belgian authorities. This was not true, but Spicer-Simson fired Lee anyway. He then had to suffer the locals singing the praises of Lee and his hunting exploits every inch of the way.

The boats were taken 2,300 miles by rail to a railhead north of Elizabethville, now Lubumbashi, in the Belgian Congo. From there, they had to be hauled 150 miles over the Mitumba Mountains, which rose to 6,400 feet and were unexplored since the days of Livingston and Stanley. Two traction engines were used to transport them down roads hacked through the jungle. The men went without washing, and sometimes without drinking water, to keep up steam and the traction engines on the road. Behind them a train of African bearers stretched for two miles.

Fearing that the traction engines might find themselves stuck in the mud when the autumn rains began, forty-two oxen were requisitioned to assist. As it was they were nearly consumed in a forest fire, a fate averted by the frantic cutting of a firebreak. The boats were then sailed four hundred miles down the Lualaba River with barrels lashed under them to reduce their draft. Back on the train again, they were taken the last bit of the way to the Belgian port of Lukuga by rail.

The African sun seems to have got to Spicer-Simson. On the way, his stories had become more and more far-fetched. He even claimed to have sunk a German cruiser, though he had lost his destroyer long before the war broke out. At Lukuga, he hung an admiral's flag outside his mud hut and took to wearing a skirt. Sometimes it was a grass skirt, otherwise a skirt his wife had made out of canvas. This caused the bemused Belgians to call him '*le commandant à la jupe*' ('the commander in a skirt'). Instead, he insisted they call him, puzzlingly, '*mon colonel*'. Even more bizarrely, when his men hung up Christmas decorations, Spicer-Simson screamed, 'What is this? A whorehouse?' and demanded that they be taken down and burnt.

When the *Kingani* came to investigate the rumours that the British had a flotilla on the lake, *Mimi* and *Toutou* set out after her. A shot from *Mimi*'s six-pounder killed the *Kingani*'s captain and two of his crew, while noncombatants watched the battle from the cliffs as if it were a cricket match. The British captured the *Kingani* and promptly ran her aground. She was refloated, repaired and renamed HMS *Fifi*. Spicer-Simson celebrated the capture by having the dead captain's ring finger cut off. He wore the captain's ring and kept the finger in a bottle.

Spicer-Simson's eccentric behaviour endeared him to the local Ba Holo Holo people. They watched as, twice a week, he bathed in public, a ceremony undertaken while he smoked a cigarette and sipped vermouth. They were fascinated by his tattoos and called him '*Bwana Chifungatumbo*' – Lord of the Loincloth – after the bath towel he wore around his waist.

The *Hedwig von Wissmann* was sent to find out what had happened to the *Kingani*. The *Fifi* took off after her but firing her twelve-pounder slowed her, and the *Wissmann* pulled away. The *Mimi* then went into action. A shot from her three-rounder slowed the *Wissmann*, and the *Fifi* caught up. By that time the *Fifi* was down to her last three shells. One jammed in her gun. It took twenty minutes before it could be cleared. The second shell knocked out the *Wissmann*'s engine room and the third sank her – but not before her naval ensign had been retrieved, the first battle flag to be captured during the war. Spicer-Simson, who had remained on deck, was now worshipped as a god by the Ba Holo Holo. Fetishes in wood and clay, showing a man with a beard, helmet and skirt, appeared for miles up and down the lake shore.

However, by then, there was another German gunboat on Lake Tanganyika. This was the 1,575-ton passenger ferry *Graf von Götzen*, armed with a 4.1-inch gun from the

SMS *Königsberg*, which had been sunk by the British in the Rufiji River in May 1915. When she turned up off Lukuga, Spicer-Simson refused to take her on. Instead he headed off down the River Congo, saying he was going to find a ship that could rival the *Götzen*. He found one in the shape of the *St George*, a steel boat belonging to the British consul at Banana, and had her dismantled and dragged to Lake Tanganyika, where she was to be reassembled.

By the time, Spicer-Simson returned to the Lukuga three months later, the situation had changed considerably. Spicer-Simson refused to participate in any further Anglo-Belgian action at the northern end of the lake in case it might involve a confrontation with the *Götzen*. Instead, he took his little flotilla to the south, where the Rhodesians were preparing an attack on Bismarckburg, now Kasanga. Even though they mocked his skirts, Spicer-Simson was charged with preventing the German garrison escaping across the lake – a task he singularly failed to perform. When reprimanded, he retired to his bed, then returned to England on sick leave. Meanwhile, the Belgians attacked the *Götzen* with seaplanes. She was stripped of her armaments and scuttled.

When news of the victory in the Battle of Tanganyika reached Europe, Spicer-Simson was awarded the Distinguished Service Order and the Belgian Order of the Crown. He had failed to sink the *Götzen*, he said, only because she had refused to come out and fight. However, stories of his less-than-heroic deeds gradually filtered back to London and Spicer-Simson was returned to his desk job.

Before the *Götzen* was sunk, her engines were covered in

a thick layer of grease. She was salvaged in 1924. Returned to service in 1927 as the MV *Liemba*, she remains in service as a ferry to this day.

Baltic baloney

Winston Churchill came up with a number of harebrained strategies during the Second World War. One of the maddest was Operation Catherine – an attempt to occupy the Baltic he thought up when first lord of the Admiralty in 1939. It was named for Catherine the Great, Empress of Russia. Churchill's plan was to rob Germany of the iron ore it brought in from Sweden and encourage the Scandinavian countries and Russia to join the Allied cause – even though the Soviet Union had signed a nonaggression pact with Germany.

The naval task force would comprise three R-class ships, HMS *Royal Sovereign*, *Revenge* and *Resolution*, and fifteen minesweepers to clear a way through the heavily mined straits between Denmark and Sweden. As the ships would be particularly vulnerable to attack by submarines and aircraft, they would be given an extra two thousand tons of armour. This would reduce their speed to a snail's pace, so other weight savings would have to be made. Two of their gun turrets would be removed and replaced with mock-ups – with tree trunks painted battleship grey masquerading as their fifteen-inch guns.

The problem was that the steel required for the armour plating was needed to build new tanks. The slow 'armoured turtles' would still be vulnerable to attack by surface ships.

Besides, the *Royal Sovereign*, *Revenge* and *Resolution* were needed to take on the German navy in the Atlantic and the North Sea. Churchill shelved Operation Catherine in January 1940 and cancelled it altogether when he became prime minister in May.

Dakar daftness

Churchill came up with an even dafter plan in June 1940 – Operation Menace. With the capitulation of France, Churchill planned to land the leader of the Free French, Brigadier-General Charles de Gaulle, at Dakar to rally the French overseas colonies to the Allied cause. De Gaulle was convinced that the forces in Dakar would welcome him with open arms. Just in case they did not, Churchill would send a task force of ten destroyers, five cruisers, two battleships and an aircraft carrier under Vice-Admiral John Cunningham. As the installation of de Gaulle had to look like a French operation, the British fleet would stay over the horizon, though British planes would be used to drop propaganda. Little resistance was expected, as Dakar harbour had little in the way of fortification. Or at least so the British thought. The most up-to-date maps the War Office could supply were published in 1919.

As the French Navy at Toulon was in the hands of the new government at Vichy that was collaborating with the

Germans, the operation needed absolute secrecy to succeed. However, French officers meeting in the Écu de France restaurant in Jermyn Street, toasted 'de Gaulle' and 'Dakar'. De Gaulle himself ordered tropical kit from Simpsons of Piccadilly, telling the sales assistant that he needed it for West Africa. Others bought maps.

As de Gaulle and his party were given a huge send-off at Euston, a case tipped off a trolley and burst open. Out spilled hundreds of leaflets carrying the French tricolour, headed *Aux Habitants de Dakar* and signed by de Gaulle. These were handed around in the pubs of Glasgow as the task force mustered in the Clyde.

As the enemy now could hardly fail to know of the operation, it was important that it proceed with all speed. However, the stores had been loaded on the French transports in no particular order. As an amphibious invasion might be called for, at the very least, the guns, which were scattered throughout the cargo, needed to be located. That took three days. The Free French forces then demanded the three months' back pay they were owed, and insisted that champagne and pâté de foie gras be added to their rations.

When the fleet sailed, Captain Poulter, who had been a liaison officer in Dakar before the war, pulled out an up-to-date map, showing the fortifications added over the previous twenty years. He also pointed out that no one in Dakar was pro-de Gaulle, only to be dismissed as a Jeremiah.

The French transports made only eight knots, not the twelve knots the British had been led to expect. Two collided and had to put in at Liverpool for repair, adding

146

further delay. Not that the British troops, under Major-General Noel Allen, minded much. Their troop ships were former liners yet to be converted, so they were served tea in their cabins by white-coated waiters and fed five-course meals. De Gaulle even had the chefs run up a special cake made with the words '*À la Victoire*' inscribed in pink icing.

Meanwhile, alerted to the British intentions, the Vichy government sent their own task force. Admiral Sir Dudley North, stationed at Gibraltar, saw it sail by and, unaware of its intentions, signalled, '*Bon voyage.*' For security reasons, he had not been briefed about the Dakar expedition. However, when the British consul at Tangiers reported sighting the French fleet to Whitehall, North was ordered to send the battle cruiser HMS *Repulse* in pursuit. Built in 1916, the *Repulse* had little chance of catching them. Even if she had, there was little she could do against three modern French cruisers, twenty years her junior. Besides, Dakar was already defended by the battleship *Richelieu*, which had been launched in 1939.

When the British task force put in at Freetown, Sierra Leone, even the Africans who paddled out in canoes knew they were on their way to Dakar. Nevertheless, the fleet hid over the horizon as ordered, while a Free French sloop carrying the Cross of Lorraine and de Gaulle's emissary sailed into the harbour. However, the authorities there were pro-Vichy and rabidly anti-British. They refused even to speak to de Gaulle's envoy. A policeman tried to arrest them and, as they made their escape, the *Richelieu* lowered one of its 380mm guns, ready to blow them out of the water. They were saved by a Free French naval bugler who sounded '*attention*'. As the gun crew snapped to attention, the sloop escaped into the fog that had now fallen.

Then the British started shelling. The intention was to knock out the French ships and destroy the city's fortifications by setting fire to the piles of groundnuts stacked around the harbour. In the fog, it proved impossible to hit the French ships, and the groundnuts refused to ignite, even when attacked by planes from the *Ark Royal*. However, a shell did hit the *Cumberland*, which returned to the Gambia for repairs.

The Free French attempted a landing, but this was called off when de Gaulle said he did not want Frenchmen spilling each other's blood. The Fleet Air Arm then tried to bomb the *Richelieu*. But the 250-pound bombs it dropped were as effective, one pilot said, as dropping bricks on the battleship's armour. But the *Richelieu* had problems of its own. The first shell it fired in anger blew back, knocking out two other guns. The propellant charge had been too high. In subsequent shells, it was lowered, but this also cut the shell's range. In a gun battle with HMS *Barham*, the *Richelieu* scored no hits, while being struck itself by one fifteen-inch round that did little damage. The *Barham* was hit twice by coastal batteries, though emerged largely unscathed – while the only damage caused to the *Devonshire* came from the cigarettes de Gaulle stubbed out on her deck.

The submarine *Bévéziers* was also in the harbour at Dakar. It was named after the Battle of Bévéziers – known to the British as the Bay of Beachy Head – a rare French naval victory in 1690. The *Bévéziers* slipped out of port, under the command of Captain Lancelot, and torpedoed

HMS *Resolution*. By then Cunningham had had enough. He withdrew, towing the *Resolution* back to Freetown.

Heads had to roll for this humiliation, so, despite his protests, Admiral North was, totally unjustly, relieved of duty. He was a scapegoat.

Later in the war, Captain Lancelot changed sides and served under Admiral Cunningham. At an awards ceremony, while Cunningham was pinning a medal on the Frenchman's chest, Lancelot admitted being the man who torpedoed the crippled *Resolution*. Cunningham's response was merely, 'Good shot.'

After the war, General Irwin paid another visit to Dakar, where he was told that it was impossible for de Gaulle ever to have imagined that the senior generals and admirals on shore would surrender to a junior officer. De Gaulle, of course, went on to become the saviour of his country.

CHAPTER SIX

Fearless Foes

 N THE GREAT IMPERIAL ENTERPRISE, the English had come up with some fabulously fearless foes, though they often managed to best them with a mixture of guile, low cunning and superior technology. The English themselves can occasionally be fearless, but that is usually characterised as foolhardy.

The Highland Dis-Charge

At the Battle of Prestonpans in 1745, the blood-curdling Highland Charge that the Scots had been using since Bannockburn in 1314 sent the English running like rabbits once again. Charles Edward Stuart – Bonnie Prince Charlie, the Young Pretender – then headed south to reclaim the throne taken from his grandfather James II by the Glorious Revolution of 1688. Although few English people rose up to support him, he met no opposition. But at Swarkestone Bridge in Derbyshire his men got cold feet and decided to return to Scotland.

They were pursued by an English army under the Duke of Cumberland, the second son of George II. He was an incompetent general who won only one battle. However, while fighting on the Continent, he had learnt a tactic introduced by the Swedish king, Gustavus II Adolphus, often known as the 'Father of Modern Warfare', a hundred years earlier. At Culloden, he lined up his men in three ranks. The front rank were ordered not to fire until the Highlanders were only twelve yards away. While the front rank reloaded, the second rank fired their guns. By the time the third rank had fired, the first rank were ready to aim and fire again. Cumberland's infantry also had the technological advantage. They were armed with new firelocks, which were faster to reload than the old matchlocks.

At Culloden, for once, the English did not turn tail and run at the sight of the Highland Charge. Instead, they stood their ground and the Scots were cut down by their rapid fire. The new guns were also fitted with bayonets, so, even if some of the enemy were able to reach the Hanoverian front-lines, they were able to defend themselves against the broadswords of the Highlanders – some of whom even resorted to throwing stones.

The Jacobites lost more than a thousand men; the redcoats lost fifty. Charles Stuart fled back to France, where the major Catholic powers repudiated his title to the British throne. He died in Rome in 1788, a drunken and broken

man. Cumberland went on to ravage the Highlands, where to this day he is remembered as a butcher. A flower was named after him to commemorate his victory at Culloden. In England it is known as the Sweet William; in Scotland it is known as the Stinking Billy.

Russia rules the waves

After Nelson's victory at Trafalgar in 1805, Britannia was set to rule the waves. Admiral Sir John Duckworth had missed the battle because he had insisted on waiting for his band, a quartet of fiddlers. However, he scored a great victory over the French at San Domingo in 1806.

The following year, Duckworth was sent to disarm or seize the Turkish fleet to prevent it attacking Britain's ally Russia. Without waiting for the Russian fleet, Duckworth fearlessly set off with seven battleships and two frigates to take on the twelve battleships and nine frigates of the Turkish fleet moored off Constantinople. Duckworth's hundred-gun flagship *Royal George* sailed through the Dardanelles, while Sir Sidney Smith on board *Pompée* captured Turkish ships that lay there, drove others aground and sent a party ashore to spike the guns.

Off Constantinople, Duckworth demanded the surrender of the rest of the Turkish fleet. Before he set off on the expedition, Admiral Collingwood, Nelson's second-in-command at Trafalgar, told Duckworth not to bother negotiating with the Turks. Give them thirty minutes to make up their minds, then, if they did not surrender, sink them, was Collingwood's counsel. Duckworth ignored this advice and sent a note giving the Turks thirty-six hours to come to a decision, but the sultan refused even to let his envoy land.

Duckworth sent another note, this time giving them just thirty minutes to comply. The Turks ignored it. He then sent a note telling them not to strengthen their shore batteries. They did just that. Duckworth then threatened to bombard Constantinople, but the Turks ambushed a longboat from HMS *Endymion*, seizing a midshipman and four ordinary seamen.

With the Turkish shore batteries almost ready to fire on the British fleet, Duckworth sent a squad of marines ashore to stop them. They were seen off with thirty casualties by the feared Turkish Janissaries. It was plain that the Turks possessed more bottle than Duckworth had and he had no alternative but to withdraw. This was easier said than done now that the batteries in the narrows at the Dardanelles had been reinforced. The Turks had not just thirty-two-pounders like the *Royal George*, but huge guns that could fire massive thousand-pound stone balls designed to crush sixteenth-century galleys. One crashed into Duckworth's flagship; another hit the *Standard*.

On the way out of the Dardanelles, Duckworth met the Russian fleet he was supposed to have waited for. As he headed back to Gibraltar with his tail between his legs, the Russians ambushed the Turkish fleet as it emerged into the Mediterranean and rescued the five British sailors the Turks had taken.

Close shave

Under exceptional circumstances an ordinary Englishman can show a fearlessness unmatched by any foe. During a charge at Ladysmith, Major Aubrey Woolls-Sampson of the Imperial Light Horse spotted one of his men lying on the ground and immediately ordered him to get up and advance. The man said that he was willing to do so. However, he was paralysed with fear. Soon after, the same man charged past the major at full pelt. Asked about his change of heart, the soldier showed him where his moustache and part of his upper lip had been shot away. The trooper yelled, 'Where are the bastards? Let me at them!' Then he steamed on and, for the rest of the action, he led the charge.

Your country needs you

In the early years of the First World War, Lord Kitchener became almost the embodiment of Britain's fighting spirit with the famous recruiting poster on which he points at the viewer and says, 'Your country needs you.' But his reputation rested on his victory at the Battle of Omdurman in the Sudan in 1897, a battle where he had made a series of near-catastrophic mistakes.

Trained as an engineer, Kitchener made a name for himself as a surveyor. He then took a number of administrative positions, seeing little action before going to the Sudan as an intelligence officer with the relief column to rescue General Gordon, whom he knew, in 1885. Gordon died in Khartoum at the hands of the Dervishes before the relief column arrived. But Kitchener stayed in the Middle East and worked his way up to become commander-in-chief of the Egyptian Army.

In 1896, he set out to reinvade the Sudan and revenge Gordon. This was to be no dashing cavalry excursion. It took him two years to reach his objective, constructing a railway across the Nubian Desert on the way. The Mahdi, who had stirred the Dervishes against Gordon, was now dead, but his successor, the caliph, sent an army of fifteen thousand men north to meet Kitchener. The caliph's camp at Atbara was defended by trenches and lines of thorn bushes. Nevertheless, it took Kitchener and fourteen thousand men just fifteen minutes to take it at bayonet point.

Kitchener then marched on the caliph's capital at Omdurman. On the way he stopped for another three months on the Nile, waiting for a fleet of gunboats to bring another eleven thousand men and more guns. Kitchener had never even commanded this many men on the parade ground, let alone in the field.

Nearing Omdurman, Kitchener blew up the Mahdi's tomb and threw his bones in the Nile, retaining the skull as an inkwell. Queen Victoria was outraged when she heard of the desecration and told him to put it back. The bones, though, could not be recovered.

At dawn on 2 September 1898, cavalry patrols reported that fifty thousand Dervishes were on their way. Kitchener established a fortified camp and his field pieces, and the gunboats began to bombard the approaching army, causing huge casualties. At a distance of a mile, the British opened up with their modern rifles. As the Dervishes moved close, the Egyptians and Sudanese troops joined in with older weaponry. Finally, the machine guns cut down the advancing tribesmen. None of the Dervishes reached closer than five hundred yards. With several thousand tribesmen dead in the sand, all Kitchener could think of saying was, 'What a dreadful waste of ammunition?'

The only casualties on the British side had been caused by Kitchener himself. Instead of ordering the British troops to dig in, he had them stand shoulder to shoulder like troops in an eighteenth-century set-piece battle. Some were hit by stray bullets. The British officers with the Egyptian and Sudanese troops had ordered their men to dig trenches; not one was injured.

Kitchener then ordered the delighted Colonel Martin of the 21st Lancers to pursue the survivors. The 21st were always being derided as the only regiment without any battle honours. Martin was determined to put this right. He ordered a charge. Four hundred men galloped across the desert at a line of Dervishes, only to find they had run into a trap. Some two thousand Dervishes were lying hidden in a wadi. Five officers, 65 men and 119 horses were killed or wounded before they could extricate themselves, the biggest loss of the battle. With the 21st was a young war correspondent named Winston Churchill, who almost lost his life. This was the last major cavalry charge in English history.

Having deprived himself of cavalry scouts, Kitchener set off to take the city, presenting his flanks to the two armies the caliph still had in the field, which outnumbered his men almost two to one. As the column stretched out across the desert, forty thousand Dervishes attacked the brigade at the rear under Brigadier-General Hector MacDonald from both sides. MacDonald stood his ground and sent a message to Kitchener. Kitchener's initial response was to order MacDonald to close up, but one of his brigadiers persuaded him to send two brigades back to help MacDonald, who had largely taken care of the situation himself by then. Kitchener scarcely even bothered to look back. When he did, he remarked only that the natives had been given a 'jolly good dusting'.

The Dervishes had lost nearly eleven thousand dead on the battlefield. Some sixteen thousand more were wounded. Many would die from gangrene. Kitchener then issued orders telling his men to shoot any tribesman who looked dangerous. Victorious troops sprayed bullets all over the place. The gunboats joined in and the *Times* war correspondent Hubert Howard was killed. He was just twenty-seven.

Kitchener returned home to a hero's welcome. In *With Kitchener to Khartoum, Daily Mail* journalist G. W. Steevens portrayed him as a man of destiny. The government gave him a £30,000 bonus and he was created Baron Kitchener of Khartoum.

The Mad Mullah

But the Dervishes had the last laugh. In 1913, against all advice, Colonel Richard Corfield took the 110 men of the British Somaliland Camel Constabulary out to face

Mohammed Abdullah Hassan, known to the British as the 'Mad Mullah'. Hassan had an army of around two thousand Dervishes, while Corfield was joined by two thousand riflemen from pro-British tribes and six hundred spearmen. He also had a Gatling gun.

At Dul Maboda in northwest Somalia, Corfield spotted Hassan's camp one evening. However, when the sun rose the next day, it seemed that the Dervishes were already on the move. A dust cloud was spotted, and Captain G. H. Summers reported that Dervish horsemen were attacking. It turned out that the dust he had seen was kicked up by stampeding ostriches.

When the Dervishes were seen advancing, Corfield formed his men into a square to fend off the attackers. But no attack came. So he decided to move his men through a patch of dense bush onto open ground where the Gatling gun would have a clear field of fire. His men were halfway through this manoeuvre when the Dervishes came down on them. His native contingent promptly deserted, taking twenty-five of the Camel Corps and the ammunition with them. The Gatling gun was struck by a stray bullet and put out of action. Trying to get it going again, Corfield was killed. Summers, who was wounded, took over, forming his men into a circle behind a ring of dead camels.

The Camel Corps were reduced to just forty men when, suddenly, for no discernible reason, the Dervishes broke off the attack, leaving six hundred dead on the battlefield. They were subdued only when the British bombed their stronghold of Taleh and the fleeing Mad Mullah died of influenza in 1920.

King Chaos

The next time Kitchener saw action – this time in South Africa – he caused a catastrophe. In 1900, the main Boer army, forty thousand men under General Cronje, had established a laager on the Modder River at Paardeberg. Facing them were fifteen thousand men under Field Marshal Lord Roberts. But Roberts came down with a chill and, as his replacement, appointed Lieutenant-General Kitchener over Major-General Thomas Kelly-Kenny.

Kelly-Kenny suggested using artillery to bombard the Boers into surrender. Kitchener dismissed this out of hand and ordered an infantry assault. The men were to ford a river and make a frontal attack on well-entrenched Boer positions. This tactic had proved suicidal twice before in South Africa. But Kitchener was sure of success.

'We'll be in the laager by half past ten,' he said.

The British infantry were marched two miles across an open plain in full view of the Boers, who were hidden in trenches and up trees. As they neared the laager, the redcoats were cut down by a sheet of rifle fire. The few survivors threw themselves to the ground for cover. So Kitchener sent in a second wave. The same thing happened. Casualties mounted and no one had yet got closer than two hundred yards from the riverbank.

Kitchener then began galloping about the battlefield issuing orders to anyone who would listen, quickly earning the nickname 'King Chaos' or 'Kitchener of Chaos' instead of Kitchener of Khartoum.

General Colville was mystified to see his Highland

Brigade making for the river when he had told them to stay where they were. But Kitchener had intervened, riding up to give verbal orders to a junior officer before galloping off again. All Colville could do was watch as his men wheeled round and marched towards the river to be cut down like his comrades.

Convinced that the men were not trying hard enough, Kitchener called up the half-battalion that were guarding the baggage train. Horrified that these men would be sacrificed too, Colville ordered them to have their lunch so that, at least, they would die with their bellies full. But Kitchener galloped up, cancelled lunch and ordered them into the attack.

Kelly-Kenny prevented Kitchener squandering the rest of the foot on the grounds that both their divisional commanders were injured. Kelly-Kenny's own men were protected, as he was suffering from dysentery and could not lead his men in to battle. Instead, Colonel Hannay's mounted infantry were ordered to take the laager at all costs. They were shot down before they got within two hundred yards of the Boer trenches. The Boers even felt sorry for them, but had no choice but to shoot.

With all Kitchener's galloping about, he seemed to have missed the fact that, on the right wing, Brigadier Smith-Dorrien had crossed the river and was now awaiting further orders. They sat there for nine hours. Then, suddenly, Smith-Dorrien saw the right wing of his brigade get up and advance on the laager, though he had given no order. Kitchener had struck again. And, again, none got closer to the laager than three hundred yards.

At sunset, the action ceased and Kitchener reported back to Field Marshal Roberts that the day had not been an unmitigated success. But he was sure that more of the same the following day would produce the desired result. Already 24 officers and 279 men had been killed, and 900 wounded.

Roberts felt much better the next day and resumed command. After assessing the situation, he took Kelly-Kenny's advice and began an artillery bombardment. The Boers surrendered two days later. But not before Kitchener had given the British their biggest single defeat in the Boer War.

Nevertheless his star was still in the ascendancy. Kitchener succeeded Roberts as commander-in-chief in South Africa in November 1900. During the last eighteen months of the war, he combated the Boers' guerrilla resistance by burning their farms and herding their wives and children into disease-ridden concentration camps. On returning to England, he was made Viscount Kitchener. Later he was promoted Field Marshal and give an earldom and another viscountcy and barony.

A great many soldiers were grateful that, at the outbreak of the First World War, he was made secretary of state for war, rather than given a field command. Nevertheless, he was as clear-sighted as Sir John French and Douglas Haig about the need to waste men's lives. He told colleagues who were expecting a short war that the war would be decided by the last million men Britain could throw into the conflict. And he quickly began recruiting.

CHAPTER SEVEN

Misguided Gallantry

ILITARY MEN OFTEN LOOK BACK to a golden age of gallantry. Magnificent though this can appear, it generally indicates a lack of forward thinking and leads to a catastrophic slaughter on the battlefield. It must be accepted that the age of chivalry is now dead.

All at sea

At the beginning of the Hundred Years' War, the French had a powerful fleet, which they could have used to invade England. Instead, in 1340, they chose to fight a battle off Sluys on the coast of Flanders that was essentially a medieval land battle fought at sea.

As the small English fleet under Edward III arrived off Flanders, the Genoese Admiral Barabavera told his French allies to put out to sea, where their greater number of ships and their greater size would give them the advantage. Instead, the French lashed their ships together to give them a platform where they could stage a pitched battle. This robbed them of any manoeuvrability.

The English ships simply sailed round to the windward side and rained arrows down on them, with English archers and their longbows outshooting the French crossbowmen, as they did at the Battle of Crécy six years later.

Once they had cleared the windward ships, English archers could board them, then climb the masts and rigging and shoot down on the French. Many of the Frenchmen preferred to jump into the water and drown rather than be shot down on board.

It was said that the French lost thirty thousand men. The defeat was so bad that no one dared tell the king. It was left up to a jester, who quipped that the French were braver than the English because they jumped into the water while the English stayed safely on their ships.

The flower of chivalry

In the Middle Ages, wars were fought to a strict code of chivalry, particularly by the French. But, in 1346, they had a surprise coming. That July the English King Edward III and his son, Prince Edward, the Black Prince, landed at Cherbourg. They were heading for Rouen when they heard that Philip VI of France was massing an army near Paris. Alongside Philip were three other kings – James II of Mallorca, Charles, King of the Romans, and blind King John of Bohemia, who had a knight chained either side of him to guide him into battle. With them were the flower of Continental chivalry, some twelve thousand knights from

France, Germany, Spain and Bohemia. The English had just 2,700 men-at-arms. However, they had eight thousand archers. But to the French knights, these were social inferiors, no-account foot soldiers.

With the bridges across the Seine cut, Edward moved his army north to retreat into Flanders. But his way was blocked by the River Somme. Now, with a massive French army on his tail, he eventually made a crossing near Blanchetaque. Then he turned to face the French outside the village of Crécy.

Vastly outnumbered, Edward deployed his army for a defensive battle. On the left he had three thousand archers, a thousand dismounted knights and some Welsh foot soldiers. On the right, near Crécy itself, there were another three thousand archers, a thousand men-at-arms and a thousand Welsh infantry. Behind them on a ridge were a reserve of two thousand archers and seven hundred dismounted knights. Eleven thousand in all, they faced a French army of *sixty* thousand.

The French foot soldiers had been marching for eighteen hours when they spotted the English at around six in the evening. Philip wanted to make camp, but the knights, who had been riding, were eager to join battle. They cried out 'Kill! Kill!' giving the impression that battle had already begun. Unable to restrain his men, Philip decided to attack.

The French were to be led into battle by six thousand crossbowmen from Genoa. They were followed by a line of knights under the command of the Count of Flanders and Count Charles II of Alençon, the king's brother. As they approached the English, the Genoans loosed off their first volley, which fell short. As they began to reload, they were hit by a storm of English arrows. Some sixty thousand rained down in the next sixty seconds.

Pounded by rocks and boulders from English catapults, the Genoans turned and ran. The fleeing crossbowmen blocked the knights' advance and Philip ordered his knights to kill them. The English were then treated to the sight of the French slaughtering their own mercenaries, while being pummelled by English arrows. When the French knights finally turned on the enemy, few were left and they made little impact on the English lines. By nightfall, the French had made fifteen charges, to no avail. More than 1,500 French men-at-arms lay dead, along with countless foot soldiers. Among the dead, were the Counts of Alençon and Flanders – and, not surprisingly, the blind King of Bohemia.

The French did not learn their lesson. Ten years later the Black Prince was leading some seven thousand men on a raid from Bordeaux into Central France. They were pursued by a French force of more than 35,000 led by Philip's successor, John II. The English turned to fight in the thickets and marshes south of Poitiers. Forgetting the lessons of Crécy, the French sent in their heavily armed knights, who became bogged down in the mud, making them easy targets for the English bowmen. King John and his son Philip were captured, along with seventeen lords, thirteen counts, and five viscounts. The French suffered 2,500 dead and wounded, and 2,000 captured. The Black Prince reported casualties of just forty dead.

Dismounted knights

By 1415, the French had learnt that the day of the mounted knight was over, but their noblemen went in with knightly decorum on foot. Henry V was then king of England and he laid claim to the French throne. After landing eleven thousand men in Normandy in August, he captured Harfleur the following month. By then, he had lost nearly half his troops, largely due to disease. They headed for Calais, hoping to sail back to England, but they were stopped by a huge French force near the village of Agincourt – now Azincourt – in the Pas-de-Calais.

Henry had some five thousand archers and nine hundred men-at-arms; the French fielded between twenty and thirty thousand men, including ten thousand knights. Chivalrously, the French chose a battlefield that would hamper the larger French force manoeuvring. It was flanked by two woods a thousand yards apart and prevented them from outflanking the English.

The battle lines formed up in sight of each other, around a thousand yards apart. They were separated by a ploughed field that was muddy after days of rain. Henry had only enough men-at-arms to form a single line. The archers were formed up on the wings, raked forward so that they could provide flanking fire. They were protected by thickets of eight-foot-long pointed stakes hammered into the ground and angled forward to impale charging French horsemen.

The French men-at-arms formed three lines. The two front lines were dismounted and carried lances cut down for fighting on foot. The rear line remained mounted. As every French nobleman wanted to be seen in the front rank and have his banner prominently displayed, the archers and crossbowmen were out to the flanks.

As the English were essentially trapped, the French delayed the attack for five hours. Henry waited, too, knowing any attack would be costly. He also knew that he had to fight that day. The English had no food and they would only get weaker, so he gave the order to advance to within three hundred yards of the French position, where the archers hammered their stakes in again. At that distance a flight of arrows is not very effective, but the first volley produced a thunderous noise when it hit French armour. This was enough to pique the cavalry into charging. The dismounted knights followed across the muddy field.

In the forty seconds it took the French horse to reach the English lines, the archers loosed off another six flights of arrows, each more deadly, as the French got closer. With the woods preventing a flanking attack, the French horse had to make a frontal assault, with the riders behind pushing those in front onto the English stakes.

Shying from the hail of arrows, the cavalry turned inwards, onto the dismounted men-at-arms, who were making slow progress over the muddy ground. As they closed, the English archers were able to fire into their flanks using arrows tipped with 'bodkin points', specially designed to penetrate armour.

As the French advanced on the English position, the field narrowed by 150 yards, compressing the French line. Arrows from English archers on the flanks compressed it further. By the time the men-at-arms arrived at the English line, they did not have enough room to wield their weapons. Sheer weight of numbers pushed the English back. But the French men-at-arms then slipped in the mud or fell over each other. In full armour, once you were down it was difficult to get up again.

With the battle joined, the French artillery, archers and crossbowmen had no clear line of fire, while English archers could pour arrows into the crush of French knights. More piled in and many were crushed to death. At Henry's signal, the archers dropped their bows to finish off the French knights with swords and axes. With the first two French lines either killed or taken prisoner, the third line of mounted men refused to attack.

By early afternoon, the prisoners taken outnumbered the entire English army, but the battle was not yet over. Fearing the prisoners were a threat to his rear, Henry ordered them to be killed. The English men-at-arms refused, so Henry picked out two hundred of his archers – tough, professional soldiers – and threatened to hang them if they did not obey his order. Within minutes two thousand men-at-arms lay dead, along with some ten thousand killed in the fighting. Ten members of the nobility were dead. Another five survived captivity. The English lost fewer than 450.

However, this left the English with an unshakeable belief
in the longbow. But it did not
reign supreme for ever. At the
Battle of Formigny in 1450
and the Battle of Castillon in
1453, the French cut down the
English archers with cannons
and small arms, giving them

victory in the Hundred Years' War and forcing the English
out of France, except for a foothold around Calais that was
relinquished in 1558.

The spoils of war

Not all beastliness takes place on the battlefield. After
Napoleon had been sent away to Elba, Wellington went to
Paris, where he sought out two of Napoleon's mistresses,
whom he bedded. One of them Josephina Grassini, was
an opera singer when Napoleon had first set eyes on her
in Milan in 1797, when he was still being faithful to his
first wife Joséphine. Three years later, he succumbed. She
mocked him for his previous indifference, saying: 'I was in
the full glory of my beauty and talents. I was the only topic
of conversation; I blinded all eyes and inflamed every heart.
Only the young general remained cold, and all my thoughts
were occupied by him alone. How strange it seems! When
I was still worth something, when the whole of Italy was at
my feet, when I heroically spurned all homage for a single
glance from your eyes, I could not obtain it. And now, now

you let your gaze rest upon me, today, when it is not worth-while, when I am no more worthy of you.'

But worthy she was. The day he took her as his mistress, he gave a lecture to two hundred Catholic priests on the need for morality. She became known as '*La Chanteuse de l'Empereur*' (the emperor's songstress) and followed him to Paris, where she sang an ode to the 'liberation' of Italy at Les Invalides on Bastille Day 1800 – which was the nineteenth-century Parisian equivalent of Marilyn Monroe singing 'Happy Birthday' to JFK. She also topped the bill at the celebration of Napoleon's famous victory at the Battle of Marengo that year. But, when he refused to acknowledge her as his official mistress, she took a lover, a twenty-two-year-old violinist from Bordeaux called Rode. Napoleon was magnanimous towards his love rival, though Joséphine grew jealous when he continued seeing his 'Giuseppina' even when she herself was crowned Empress. Grassini is thought to have cost the French taxpayer seventy thousand francs a year between 1807 and 1814.

Wellington became acquainted with Grassini in 1814 while Napoleon was in exile. At forty-one, she was no longer the succulent twenty-seven-year-old Napoleon had first enjoyed in Milan but, by all accounts, she was still tremendously sexy. Unlike Napoleon, Wellington did not take three years to get her into bed – even though he, too, was a married man. The British taxpayer was presented with only modest dressmaking and millinery bills. She called him *cher Villianton* and Wellington freely flaunted his trophy mistress as the composer Felice Blangini recalled:

When Madame Grassini attended informal gatherings at Lord Wellington's she declaimed and sang scenes from *Cleopatra* and *Romeo and Juliet*. Alone in the centre of the salon, she gestured as if she was on stage and using a big shawl she dressed up in different ways. I cannot remember if, during these sessions, she sang arias which end with a *sguardo d'amor* [an amorous glance]; but what I am certain of is that Lord Wellington was enchanted, in ecstasy.

The affair banished any thought she had of joining Napoleon on Elba. After Waterloo, Wellington was even more attentive. According to the Comtesse de Boigne, on one occasion, he:

> conceived the idea of making Grassini, who was then at the height of her beauty, the queen of the evening. He seated her upon a sofa mounted on a platform in the ballroom, and never left her side; caused her to be served before anyone else, made people stand away in order that she might see the dancing, and took her into supper himself in front of the whole company; there he sat by her side, and showed her attentions usually granted only to princesses. Fortunately, there were some high-born English ladies to share the burden of this insult, but they did not feel the weight of it as we did, and their resentment could not be compared with ours.

For *La Chanteuse* the beastliness should have been confined to the bedroom. Until her death in 1823, she would recall her time with Napoleon and rue, 'Why would he not listen to me and patch things up with *ce cher Villianton*?'

According to the historian Andrew Roberts, 'To sleep with one of Napoleon's mistresses might be considered an accident, but to sleep with two might suggest a pattern of triumphalism . . .' The second of Napoleon's mistresses Wellington bedded was Marguerite Joséphine Weimer. She was just fifteen going on sixteen when the thirty-three-year-old first consul seduced her. An actress, she used the stage name Mademoiselle George. He called her Georgina and once pushed forty thousand francs down her cleavage, presumably in notes.

The two-year affair rankled Joséphine, but, as Napoleon explained, 'Exclusivity is not in my nature.' Joséphine was particularly put out when he took her to see Mademoiselle George in the play *Cinna* at the Théâtre Français. In the play, La Weimer uttered the line, 'If I have seduced Cinna, I shall seduce many more.' At that point the audience rose to applaud the first consul, who was sitting in a box alongside his wife.

The affair ended in 1804. As Marguerite put it, 'He left me to become emperor.'

From 1808 until 1812, La Weimer was in Russia, where, presumably, she and Napoleon were reunited. An anecdote about her appears in the opening scene of *War and Peace*. When he abdicated in 1814, she was referred to in the press as the Corsican widow and hissed on stage.

She was twenty-seven when Wellington inherited her. Her affair with the Duke was more discreet, perhaps because Grassini was on the scene. However, she has done history the favour of comparing the performance of the two men. '*Monsieur le Duc était beaucoup le plus fort*,' she said ('The Duke was much the more virile'). This will come as a welcome relief to English readers who have long lived with the notoriously bitchy comment from another of Wellington's mistresses that one of their greatest national heroes was, in bed at least, 'a cold fish'. The French can draw comfort from the fact that Napoleon had a phalanx of Imperial bed-warmers during his marriage to Joséphine and, according to his foreign minister Armand de Caulaincourt, such affairs were only 'a distraction which afforded him but little amusement'.

After Wellington, La Weimer's fortunes went into decline. In 1855, she applied for the position of manager of the Lost Umbrella Office at the Paris Exposition, but did not get the job. She died in 1867.

As well as taking over Napoleon's mistresses, Wellington bought the house of Napoleon's famously sexy sister Pauline, where she had been carried naked every day to her bath of milk by her black servant Paul. Unfortunately, the promiscuous Pauline was not around at the time, having moved

to Rome to live under the protection of Pope Pius VII. However, Wellington kept her picture in his bedroom next to that of Grassini. Between them was a portrait of Pius VII – like 'our Lord between the two thieves,' said the Comte d'Artois. Famously depicted nude by the Italian sculptor Antonio Canova, Pauline was asked how she could possibly pose naked. She replied, 'Why not? It was not cold, there was a fire in the studio.'

Wellington also engaged Napoleon's cook, called on his sister-in-law and acquired an extensive collection of Napoleona. He even had Canova's nude statue of Napoleon, when a youthful first consul, installed in his London home, Apsley House. It cost 66,000 francs.

More beastly battles of the bedroom

A five-year study in the 1830s found that the annual rate of sexually transmitted diseases among British soldiers in India was between 320,000 and 450,000, while it only afflicted 2–3 per cent of the Indian troops. The answer was regulated regimental brothels, where the prostitutes could undergo medical inspections. However, there was a constant battle between those who wanted to keep the brothels open for health reasons and those who wanted them closed for moral reasons.

When they did close in 1888, the infection rate shot up to 371 per thousand. By the time they reopened in 1899 it had climbed to 50 per cent. Some cases were so bad that the men would have to be sent back to Britain for treatment. Between 1880 and 1900, it is estimated that ten thousand British soldiers were invalided home *hors de combat*.

In the First World War, 416,891 British soldiers were admitted to hospital suffering from a sexually transmitted disease – a quarter of all those treated for non-combat-related conditions. As each sufferer spent an average of six weeks in hospital, STDs were a considerable drain on manpower. Again, the British army experimented with brothels staffed with medically inspected prostitutes: one at Rouen accommodated 171,000 men in the first year, with only 248 reported cases of venereal disease.

During the Second World War, there were separate brothels in Tripoli for officers and men, but these were closed down by the chaplain-general, forcing soldiers to use unregulated houses. General Montgomery also closed down the regulated brothels in Egypt. One army doctor complained, 'Within three weeks every bed in the previously almost deserted VD ward, and every bed that could be crammed on to the verandah, was full.'

VD rates regularly outstripped battle casualties. During the heavy fighting in North Africa in 1941, casualties reached 3.5 per cent, while the VD rate was 4.1 per cent. Then, in Italy in 1945, the casualty rate dropped to 0.9 per cent, while the VD rate was 6.8 per cent. And in Burma in 1943, casualties stood at 1.3 per cent with a VD rate at a massive 15.7 per cent.

However, when it came to *l'amour* no one handled it as well as the French. They had run special military brothels since the 1840s. During the First World War, they offered to extend their services to the Americans, but the secretary of war declined on the grounds that, if such an arrangement reached the ears of the rather priggish President Woodrow Wilson, he might withdraw military assistance from the Allies. Unabashed, the French awarded the Croix de Guerre to two prostitutes who had held the fort in a remote outpost in Indo-China.

War as a spectator sport

The Crimean War was not all gloom and doom. Far from it. In the summer months, at least, it was a spectator sport. Pavilions were erected on the hilltops and well-dressed men and women would sip champagne and sup caviar, while the slaughter took place below.

One officer compared the spectators at the siege of Sevastopol in May 1855 to the crowds on Epsom Downs on Derby Day. There were off-duty officers picnicking, wives, pressmen, gentlemen travellers, tourists and salesmen. So many foreigners came to see the spectacle that one observer said the whole world was represented with the possible exception of North American Indians. The beautiful Lady George Paget – dubbed 'the belle of the Crimea' – was there, often accompanied by Piedmontese soldiers wearing hats decorated with plumes of black cock's feathers. Her husband, commander of the now much depleted cavalry, was on duty near at hand. By then the cavalry had already fallen so far out of favour the only role Lord Raglan could now envisage for his horsemen was to prevent a rush of souvenir hunters once Sevastopol had fallen.

But for Lady Paget there were no such cares. Regimental bands would play music more suited to a Sunday afternoon in Regent's Park. The hit of the season was a band from Sardinia who played a selection of tunes from operas. There were race meetings, bathing parties and fishing trips. The *zouaves*, exotically dressed French colonial troops from North Africa, had their own theatre company that staged a series of outrageous farces. In spite of the mud and filth of the Crimea, they always looked as smart and clean as if they had just left Paris.

The English, of course, played cricket. The day after the Battle of the Chernaya River on 16 August 1855, an eleven from the Guards Division took the field against the 'Leg of Mutton Club', a team of officers from other regiments. The players and their ladies enjoyed a hearty tea accompanied by the sound of gunfire.

Not cricket – yes, it is, actually

On the 101st day of the Siege of Ladysmith, the beleaguered Brits received a heliograph message from a Boer, who was clearly a cricket fan, saying, '101 not out.' The reply from the First Manchesters was, 'Still batting.'

Meanwhile at Mafeking, the besieged Colonel Robert Baden-Powell received a message from the Boer commander, Field Cornet Sarel Eloff, that read:

Dear Sir,
I see in the *Bulawayo Chronicle* that your men in Mafeking play cricket on Sundays, and give concerts and balls on Sunday evenings. In case you will allow my men to join in, it would be very agreeable to me, as here, outside Mafeking, there are seldom any of the fair sex, and there can be no merriment without them being present. In case

you would allow this we could spend some of the Sundays, which we still have to get through round Mafeking, and of which there will probably be several, in friendship and unity. During the course of the week, you can let us know if you accept my proposition and I shall then, with my men, be on the cricket field, and at the ballroom at times so appointed by you. I remain,

Your obedient friend,

Sarel Eloff,

Commandant.

According to his biographer, Baden-Powell read the letter with a sardonic smile and sent his answer to the Boer lines under a white flag. It read:

Sir,

I beg to thank you for your letter of yesterday, in which you propose that your men should come and play cricket with us. I should like nothing better – after the match in which we are at present engaged is over. But just now we are having our innings and have so far scored 200 days not out against the bowling of Cronje, Snyman and Botha, and we are having a very enjoyable game.

I remain,

Yours truly,

RSS Baden-Powell

A large number of Boers learnt cricket as prisoners of war in camps on St Helena, Bermuda, Ceylon and in India. There were games between the Boers and their British captors as well as local teams. Boers from a camp at Diyatalawa, which boasted a cricket club of more than seventy, were paroled to play the Colombo Colts on the ground of the Nondescript Cricket Club in Victoria Park. They were given an enthusiastic reception by both the English and Ceylonese spectators. The Boers lost and presented the Colts an inscribed paperknife as a souvenir of the match.

Marthinus Hendrik Steyn, who was just seventeen when he was captured, was made an honorary British officer by his captors so he could tour India with the regimental team. On the other side, James Hugh Sinclair had to escape from captivity with the Boers to tour England with the South African team in 1901. In South Africa's next test series, the following year against Australia, he scored a century in eighty minutes and remains the sixth-quickest batsman to reach that target in test history.

CHAPTER EIGHT

Ridiculous Retreats

'HE WHO FIGHTS AND RUNS AWAY lives to fight another day' is a saying that can trace its roots to Athenian orator and statesman Demosthenes in 338 BC, when he dropped his weapons and fled the battlefield. It was just as true in Old England as it was in Ancient Greece.

The Canter of Coltbrigg

With the British Army deeply committed on the Continent in the War of the Austrian Succession, Britain itself was practically defenceless when Charles Edward Stuart – the Young Pretender – landed in Scotland in July 1745, fomenting the Jacobite Rebellion. By 15 September Bonnie Prince Charlie was just eight miles from Edinburgh. The city had no regular troops to defend it, except for the Thirteenth and Fourteenth Dragoons, both newly formed regiments of raw recruits.

On the morning of the 16th, they were drawn up at

Coltbridge with the town guard. A few gunshots and the appearance of some rebels on horseback sent the pickets into a panic. This soon infected the rest of the dragoons, who mounted their horses and galloped away, not stopping until they reached Prestonpans ten miles away. There they stopped for the night. But one of the dragoons went foraging after dark and fell into a disused coal pit full of water. When he yelled for help, the cry went up that the rebels had

arrived and the dragoons galloped on another twenty miles to Dunbar.

So Charles Stuart entered Edinburgh unopposed and took up residence in Holyrood House, while men from all over Scotland rallied to his cause.

Marlborough's spoons

During the Seven Years' War, Prime Minister William Pitt the Elder returned to the old policy of trying to tie down French troops by making hit-and-run raids on the Channel coast. In June 1758, the Duke of Marlborough – grandson of the first duke – had led an expedition to St Malo, but had to make such a rapid withdrawal that he left his silver spoons behind. These were graciously returned by the French commander.

Cast not a clout

After his hasty retreat from St Malo, Marlborough was sent off to command British forces in Germany and the seventy-three-year-old Lieutenant-General Thomas Bligh was put in charge of fresh raids on the French coast. In August 1758, he captured Cherbourg. The harbour and its shipping, its piers and fort were destroyed and his men plundered the city and surrounding countryside. The city's brass cannons were taken back to London, where they were paraded through the streets in triumph.

Next, Bligh had a go at St Malo to see if he could succeed where Marlborough had failed. But, while he was landing his troops, the wind suddenly changed and the fleet had to seek shelter in the Bay of St Cast, taking with it the horses and artillery. Without the guns, any attack on St Malo was impracticable. While Bligh was wondering what to do, French troops arrived, so Bligh and his men had no choice but to head for St Cast. On the way, they had to cross the River Équernon. There was no bridge there, but at low tide they could wade across. Unfortunately, when they arrived it was high tide and they had to wait the nine hours for the tide to turn. Meanwhile, more French soldiers arrived.

Reaching St Cast, Bligh decided to make camp rather than re-embark immediately. He then received intelligence that a French force of ten thousand men was on its way. Instead of slipping away at night, Bligh waited until daybreak, announcing his intentions with the drumming of reveille. He then sent his men off in single column, prolonging the evacuation. Enemy fire from the heights sank many of the boats and the departing soldiers drowned. The Grenadier Guards under Major-General Alexander Drury fought a rearguard action on the beach, but they were eventually overrun by the French. Around a thousand men were killed, wounded or captured. Drury drowned while trying to swim out to the boats.

Bligh escaped a court martial, but was snubbed at court and retired to his property in Ireland. His failure at St Malo meant that Pitt was forced to abandon his hit-and-run strategy and commit himself instead to mastery of the seas.

The Castlebar Races

With the Napoleonic War in full swing, Bonaparte attempted an invasion of Ireland in support of the Republican Wolfe Tone. However, Tone and General Jean Hardy, commanding three thousand men, were delayed in Brest by adverse winds. Meanwhile, General Amable Humbert, sailing from Rochefort with fewer than a thousand men, landed at Killala in County Mayo. When he met no resistance, General Humbert thought he ought to find a way to announce his presence.

Spotting an elegant Georgian mansion, he opened the gate and tramped up the drive. The door was answered by a servant, who fetched his master, Dr John Stock, a Protestant bishop. Humbert informed him that he had just invaded Ireland. Stock took this news with equanimity and excused himself, as he had a sermon to write.

Now that the invasion was official, Humbert marched his men to the middle of Killala and hoisted a green flag bearing the legend 'Ireland forever' and a harp. They then marched on Castlebar, attracting along the way a large force of Irish volunteers.

Even though exhausted after their march from Killala and outnumbered three to one, the French and their Irish followers put to flight four thousand British regular soldiers with artillery. The infantry retreated thirty miles to Tuam in County Galway, while the cavalry fled as far as Athlone, covering sixty-three miles in twenty-four hours. Although the French and Irish stopped chasing them after a mile or two, the retreat was so precipitous that it has been known ever after as the Castlebar Races.

However, things then began to go wrong for the invasion force. The Viceroy in Dublin, General Cornwallis – the man who had lost the American War of Independence – marched out with forty thousand men. Although Humbert had collected more Irish volunteers, they were outnumbered twenty to one and fought for thirty minutes before surrendering. Humbert was then treated to tea and cakes, while the Irish volunteers were massacred.

Soon afterwards, Irish patriot Napper Tandy sailed into Donegal harbour with 270 French soldiers. When they heard of Humbert's defeat, they got drunk and Tandy had to be carried back to the ship to return to exile.

Wolfe Tone and General Hardy set out only to have their small fleet scattered by an English squadron. Tone was captured when he landed at Lough Swilly in Donegal and taken to Dublin in chains. He managed to cut his throat in prison before he could be publicly executed.

Tone was followed by Captain Savary, who sailed from

Rochefort on 12 October with the band of the 70th Regiment. Arriving in Killala harbour, he ordered the band to play, then sailed back to France without landing.

Retreat from Kabul

The Great Game was the struggle between the expanding empires of Russia and Britain in Central Asia. As part of it, Britain invaded Afghanistan, repeatedly. In December 1838, 21,000 men under Sir John Keane set out from the Punjab. Entering Afghanistan they decisively beat Dost Mohammad, the Amir of Kabul, deposed him and installed Shah Shoja, the former king, who had been in exile in British India for twenty-eight years.

It soon became clear that the Shah's rule could be maintained only by a British occupation. General Sir Willoughby Cotton stayed in Kabul with five thousand men, while General William Nott occupied Kandahar. The British resident, or representative, William Macnaghten allowed his soldiers to bring their wives and children to Afghanistan to improve morale. The Afghans saw this as a sign that the British intended to remain indefinitely and began to rally around the exiled Dost Mohammad's son, Akbar Khan.

Blissfully unaware of local resentment, the British moved out of the fort in the centre of Kabul and into a cantonment built to the northeast of the city. It was completely indefensible. Lying on low swamp ground, it was surrounded by higher ground and forts occupied by the Afghans. The perimeter was two miles long and the stores were housed in a separate commissariat three hundred yards outside the main compound. When the strategic disadvantage of this arrangement was pointed out to General Cotton, he said he was too busy building barracks to be concerned about stores.

Cotton was replaced by Major-General William Elphinstone, who was nearly sixty and had last seen action twenty-five years before at Waterloo. On the verge of senility, he was flatulent, incontinent and so badly crippled with gout and rheumatism that he could not walk or ride and had to be carried on a litter. He declined the appointment, describing himself 'unfit for it, done up body and mind', but Lord Auckland, the Governor-General of India, insisted. Cotton reassured him, 'You will have nothing to do here, all is peace.' But, arriving in Kabul racked with pain and indecision even Elphinstone queried the defensibility of the cantonment. But any attempt at improvement was turned down on the grounds of expense.

In November 1841, the British Envoy Sir William Macnaughten's principal assistant, Sir Alexander Burnes, and his aides were murdered by a mob in Kabul. Elphinstone did nothing. As a result, the Afghans besieged the cantonment. With the commissariat in enemy hands, the British were down to three days' food. Elphinstone rallied, tried to mount his horse, fell off and was trampled. From his sickbed, he ranted about the shortage of ammunition, though they had enough to withstand a year's siege.

Elphinstone was not aided by his second-in-command, Brigadier John Shelton, who openly despised him. Shelton was a man of action who led several misguided forays out of the cantonment, only to have his men cut down by Afghan marksmen. He was no tactician, either. Ignoring standing orders that at least two field pieces must be taken into any action, Shelton headed out with one. At first, it held the Afghans at a distance. But then it became too hot to operate and they closed in. Shelton was hit five times by spent bullets and was spared only because he was forced to follow his men when they fled. Lady Sale, who watched the action, said that Shelton had not been routed by ferocious tribesmen, but rather local tradesmen.

When Elphinstone held 'councils of war' where anyone – soldier or civilian – could pitch in, Shelton brought his bedding, rolled it out on the floor and feigned sleep to show his contempt. The situation was not improved when Elphinstone was shot in the buttocks. Macnaughten figured he could negotiate a settlement, but, when he went to a meeting with Akbar Khan, he was murdered and his body dragged through the streets of Kabul.

Elphinstone then secured an agreement for the garrison to withdraw, even though it was the middle of the Afghan winter and the snow was already a foot thick. On 1 January 1842, a British contingent of sixteen thousand – twelve thousand of whom were women and children – pulled out of Kabul. They were attacked almost immediately. Women and children were butchered in the snow. Only one European, Dr William Brydon, reached the safety of the British garrison at Jalalabad.

Nineteen officers and ten wives with their children were taken into captivity as hostages. Elphinstone was among them. He had been wounded during the retreat. While the prisoners were not treated badly, Elphinstone was racked with dysentery and died. Akbar Khan had his body covered in scented leaves, wrapped in felt blankets and sent under guard to Jalalabad. But his escorts were ambushed by tribesmen, who stripped the corpse and pelted it with stones. However, the body was recovered and buried with full military honours.

Buoyed by success, Akbar Khan besieged Jalalabad, but General Sale marched out and routed him. General Pollack forced his way through the Khyber Pass to inflict another defeat on Akbar Khan. In September, the British retook Kabul, released the prisoners and burned the main bazaar in retaliation for the destruction of Elphinstone's column. Then they withdrew, only to invade again in 1878, 1919 and 2001.

Magnificent sepoys

When the First World War began, the British seized the opportunity to expand their empire in Africa. They tore up the agreement guaranteeing the neutrality of Dar es Salaam and the port of Tanga in what was then German East Africa. As the British Army was fully committed in Europe, the job of relieving Germany of her African possessions was left to the Indian Army. Command of the expeditionary force was given to Major-General A. E. Aitken, a thirty-five-year army veteran, who rated his 'magnificent' sepoys over a bunch of

'Huns' and 'Blacks' – the German-trained Askaris who made up the *Schutztruppe* under Colonel Paul Emil von Lettow-Vorbeck. However, Aitken's intelligence officer, old Africa hand Captain Richard Meinertzhagen, described Aitken's troops as 'the worst in India'.

'I tremble to think what may happen if we meet with serious opposition,' he said. 'The senior officers are nearer to fossils than active, energetic leaders.'

Aitken refused the help of the King's East African Rifles, whose commander, Lieutenant-Colonel B. R. Graham, warned that the Askaris should not be underestimated. But Aitken dismissed them as 'a bunch of niggers' who were to be thrashed by his superior Indian troops by Christmas. He needed no help from anyone who might know anything of the conditions or terrain they were going to fight in.

Prussian black

Von Lettow-Vorbeck's *Schutztruppe* knew everything about the conditions they were going to fight in. There were just 2,500 of them, divided into independent companies consisting, usually, of sixteen German officers and NCOs and 160 native Askari troops. The German troops serving in East Africa had been handpicked. The Askaris drilled with Prussian discipline and taught marksmanship with modern small arms. The Africans taught the Europeans their tactics, camouflage and survival techniques. Some Askaris rose to become senior NCOs and were put in charge of white troops, which was unheard of in those days.

While Gurkhas and the North Lancaster Regiment under

Aitken's command were indeed outstanding, most of the eight thousand Indian troops were untrained, ill equipped and poorly led. They had recently been issued with modern Lee-Enfield rifles, but had not been taught how to use them. Coming from all parts of India, the soldiers spoke twelve different languages. They followed different faiths and were led by men they had never set eyes on before they left Bombay.

The convoy had been delayed and the troops were stuck in holds of their transports for sixteen days in the appalling heat. Little thought had been given to dietary considerations required by religion and caste. Those who did not suffer from seasickness were struck down by diarrhoea caused by eating food they were unaccustomed to. It was suggested that the troops should disembark at Mombasa in British East Africa (BEA) to recover. Aitken dismissed the idea, saying that it might alert the Germans.

But von Lettow-Vorbeck already knew that the British were on their way. Crates on the dockside in Bombay had been marked 'Indian Expeditionary Force "B", Mombasa, British East Africa'. The newspapers in Britain and East Africa also announced the forthcoming arrival of the force. Mombasa's German residents wrote letters to their counterparts in the German protectorate and uncoded radio messages were transmitted between the port and the convoy. The fleet even sailed down the coast in sight of land just in case the Germans had missed it.

Let's warn the enemy

Captain F. W. Caulfield, commanding the cruiser HMS *Fox*, sailed ahead of the main force. Arriving at Tanga, Captain Caulfield went ashore to tell German District Commissioner Auracher that the neutrality treaty no longer applied and, if he did not surrender, Tanga would be bombarded. Auracher said that he would have to consult his superior, the governor, Dr von Schnee. Caulfield asked whether the harbour was mined. Auracher answered that it was, though it wasn't. Then Caulfield was forced to wait while Auracher went off, ostensibly in search of von Schnee. Instead, he raised the German flag, changed into his army uniform, gathered his fifteen-man Askari police force and went off to join von Lettow-Vorbeck.

Alerted to the imminent arrival of the British invasion fleet, von Lettow-Vorbeck rushed a force of just 250 Askaris to Tanga. Meanwhile, the British landing was further delayed by Caulfield's needless minesweeping of the harbour. Caulfield persuaded Aitken to land his men three miles further down the coast, out of sight of the still-undefended town. They landed in a mangrove swamp infested with leeches, water snakes, mosquitoes and tsetse flies. Beyond that they faced a fifty-foot rock face that they had to scale. Despite this, Aitken issued an order, saying, 'I will not tolerate the appalling sloppiness of dress allowed during the late war with the Boers.'

Nevertheless, he permitted his troops a little rest after their horrendous voyage. Meinertzhagen bedded down for the night in the garden of a house on the outskirts of Tanga on a mattress stuffed with 'nice bits of lingerie' he had found in the house, covering himself with a large German flag and a Union Jack.

Stumbling in to battle

By the time the advance began the following morning, the Germans had had forty-eight hours to prepare their defences. Even so, Aitken dispensed with any reconnaissance and ploughed ahead. His men stumbled through a cocoa plantation, causing von Lettow-Vorbeck to remark on 'the clumsiness with which the English troops were moved and led into battle'.

At first they could see no enemy, so three British officers climbed a small hill to get a better view. They were immediately shot. A German bugle sounded and the Askaris charged at the 13th Rajputs, who turned and ran, leaving their British officers to be cut down. Meinertzhagen tried to stop the rout, but an Indian officer drew his sword and had to be shot. Aitken was watching the action from the deck of one of the British ships. They had already lost three hundred men when Brigadier Tighe, commanding the Bangalore Brigade, signalled back that they were facing a force of 2,500, though in fact it was only a tenth of that number.

The Royal Navy offered a naval bombardment by the big guns of HMS *Goliath* to soften up the enemy. Having conducted no reconnaissance, Aitken had no idea where the enemy were, so he gracefully declined the naval bombardment for fear of damaging civilian property. Instead, he ordered a second attack in full strength. The Gurkhas and North Lancs would take the lead with the Indian regiments following up behind.

Phoned ahead

The *Schutztruppe* were ready for them. Defensive positions were linked by field telephones. Barbed wire had been deployed. Askaris took cover behind the solid brick and stone houses. There were snipers up trees. The crack company of Askaris, armed with the most modern rifles, flanked the British attack, while others manned Maxim guns.

The attack came at noon. In the heat, the Indian troops had already drained their water bottles and were now in a state of collapse. They were terrified by the huge plumes of smoke that issued from the old black-powder Jägerbüchse M/71 rifles issued to the Askaris. The Askaris also taunted them, shouting, 'Indians are insects.'

The Imperial Service Brigade advanced through fields of corn eight foot high. They could not see the enemy, while Askaris up the trees dispatched them with a shot to the top of the head. Nevertheless, the Gurkhas and North Lancs succeeded in routing the Askaris in the town, taking the hospital

and customs house, and raising the Union Jack. At the height of the fighting, some English sailors rowed into the harbour in an attempt to buy some food.

Battle of the Bees

In the area surrounding the town, local beekeepers suspended hollow logs in the branches of trees as hives. The African honey bee is a particular large and aggressive insect. The noise of battle, stray bullets and shrapnel disturbed them. Swarms attacked the advancing Indian soldiers. Some men suffered hundreds of stings. They panicked and raced for the safety of the sea, being stung repeatedly as they fled. This led the British to nickname the Battle of Tanga, the 'Battle of the Bees'. Later, *The Times* claimed that the underhand von Lettow-Vorbeck had deliberately used the bees as a weapon.

As men began arriving at the beach waving their arms in the air, Aitken assumed that they were being driven back by a large German force and ordered a bombardment to halt them. This stirred up the bees all the more. The bombardment was stopped when the one and only recorded hit fell on the hospital, which, by then, was filled with the British wounded and dying. Those Indians still on the battlefield were shooting wildly, doing more damage to their own side than the enemy. In one attack, the British casualties were eight hundred killed, five hundred wounded and more than a thousand missing or captured. The Germans suffered a total of sixty-nine killed and wounded.

Two more companies of Askaris arrived by train. They were still outnumbered eight to one. Due to a misunderstanding over orders and natural caution, they withdrew to a camp several miles to the west of Tanga. That night, the British could have taken the town without a fight. Instead,

Aitken was intent on re-embarking his troops, who abandoned their equipment. Von Lettow-Vorbeck was able to re-equip three Askari companies with modern rifles – for which he now had 600,000 rounds of ammunition, courtesy of the British. He also had sixteen new machine guns, motorcycles, telegraph equipment, barbed wire, tents, blankets and enough food and clothing to last the *Schutztruppe* a year.

'You regard war as a game'

The following day Captain Meinertzhagen entered Tanga under a white flag, carrying medical supplies and a letter from General Aitken, apologising for shelling the hospital. He arranged for the evacuation of the wounded and found the Germans magnanimous in victory.

'You English are really quite incomprehensible,' he was told. 'You regard war as a game.' As if to prove the point, British troops took the opportunity to go swimming in a breach of protocol the Germans found horrifying.

Back at Mombasa, the British were refused permission to land until they had paid a 5 per cent duty on their rifles. The situation was rapidly resolved when the North Lancs regiment showed the customs officials their bayonets.

Steaming Down to Tanga

Recalled to Britain, Aitken was refused an audience with the secretary of war Lord Kitchener, demoted to colonel and retired to half pay. Although Caulfield had warned the

Germans of the arrival of the British force, thus ensuring the failure of the invasion, he was promoted for his gentlemanly behaviour. The expedition was commemorated by a satirical song called 'Steaming Down to Tanga'.

Von Lettow-Vorbeck continued running rings around the British, Belgians and Portuguese in Africa until the end of the war. Despite his efforts, all Germany's possessions in Africa were ultimately ceded to the British and French. Nevertheless, when he returned to Germany in 1919, von Lettow-Vorbeck was given a hero's welcome as the only German commander to successfully invade British territory during the First World War.

Between a rock and a hard place

When the First World War began in August 1914, one of the first British units to be sent to France was the 5th Division. Attached to it was the 80th Battery of Horse Artillery. At nightfall they rode up to the village of La Cateau. The locals, seeing uniformed men speaking in a foreign language, opened fire. This sent the Horse Artillery galloping back to the British lines. However, the picket also mistook them for the enemy and opened fire. Two men were dead before the 5th Division even saw a German.

U-boat round the U-bend

During an engagement off Scotland on 13 April 1945, German submarine U-1206 made an undignified retreat to the bottom of the sea, thanks to an inexperienced seaman who chose the wrong time to go the lavatory – which could be a hazardous business while submerged. Known humorously as 'Tube 7', the early toilets could not be flushed at a depth greater than twenty-five or thirty metres, due to the water pressure, and porcelain cracks easily when subjected to shocks from depth charges. Later in the war, a lavatory that could be flushed at a greater depth was provided, but special training was needed to operate it, leading to the bogus 'water closet certificate' WC Schein. But this was no laughing matter. An ill-executed flush on U-1206 allowed waste and seawater to flood the forward compartment. The waterlogged batteries gave off chlorine gas, forcing the submarine to surface. It was then bombed and strafed. Three men were killed. The rest of the crew then abandoned ship and rowed ashore in what must have been the most embarrassing U-boat loss of the war.

CHAPTER NINE

Naval Nonsense

EASTLY BATTLES TAKE PLACE AT sea as well as on land, especially for the English. The Royal Navy is a creation of Old England. Its origins belong with Alfred the Great, often seen as the first king of England. Henry VIII and Elizabeth I developed the English Navy into a major fighting force. Charles II gave it the appellation Royal and it played a key role in the expansion of the Empire, providing plenty more beastly battles.

Hot Damme

In 1213, King Philip II of France planned to invade England and put his son Louis on the throne. He assembled a vast fleet of 1,700 ships and a huge invading army. However, before he could sail for England, he heard that his vassal Count Ferrand of Flanders had turned against him. So he sailed for Bruges instead.

Damme, on the estuary of the River Zwyn, now silted up, was then the port of Bruges. Philip left his armada there, unguarded, while he took his army to besiege Ghent. Meanwhile, a small English fleet under the Earl of Salisbury sailed from England. They pillaged the French fleet, burnt most of the ships and sacked the town. When Philip returned, he found the harbour

blocked with wreckage and burned what was left of his fleet, saying, 'The French know nothing of the sea.'

Eustace the Monk

Four years later, Philip II was still trying to invade England. But, lacking ships, he depended on Eustace the Monk, a former Benedictine monk who became a mercenary and a pirate with bases on the Channel Isles. After working for King John of England, he switched sides and began ferrying Prince Louis's troops to England and burning coastal villages.

In 1217, a large fleet under Eustace was sighted off Dover. Folkestone had recently been sacked, so Hubert de Burgh, castellan of Dover, set out with a small fleet to repel him. As de Burgh approached, the French mocked the pathetic English force, but de Burgh sailed past them, as if heading for Calais. Instead, he turned so that he was now upwind of Eustace's fleet. This meant he could pick off the leeward ships without those further downwind being able to come to their rescue.

The English also used the wind to blow quicklime into the eyes of the French before boarding their ships. Eustace's flagship was surrounded and captured. He was found hiding in the bilges and offered a huge ransom for his life. But the English refused, giving him only one choice: whether to have his head cut off on the ship's rail or on the side of the siege engine he was bringing to England as deck cargo.

Again, tales told about Eustace the Monk are similar to those told about Robin Hood, and it is thought that the renegade French monk may have been another of the models on which the English outlaw was based.

The *Mary Sank*

In July 1545, England was, yet again, at war with France and the French king François I sent a fleet under Claude d'Annebault, Admiral of France, to invade. Things did not start out well. During a state dinner on board his flagship *Carragon* to celebrate the forthcoming campaign, there was an accident in the kitchens. The ship caught fire and the magazine exploded, killing almost everyone on board, including many of the court's great ladies who had come for dinner. However, Annebault escaped and set off on *La Maîtresse*, which promptly ran aground. Undeterred he continued on the damaged ship, which then sank off the Isle of Wight. Annebault was picked up by one of his galleys.

In the sheltered waters of the Solent, the French oar-powered galleys had a distinct advantage. At the time, the English fleet of sailing ships were becalmed in Portsmouth harbour. However, as the galleys came in for the attack, the wind picked up and Henry VIII's pride and joy, the *Mary Rose*, sailed out at the head of the port division of the English fleet.

She was a formidable fighting vessel that had already proved her worth in battle in the First and Second French Wars. However, in 1536, she had been altered, increasing her weight from five hundred tons to seven hundred, maybe even eight hundred. Twenty-two guns were added. As a result she was top-heavy and unseaworthy. And, when she sailed out of Portsmouth harbour on 19 July 1545, her decks were packed with heavily armoured soldiers, making her even more unstable.

As she came about to attack the French galleys, the lower gunports were open for action. A sail being unfurled was caught by a gust of wind and they dipped under the water. The lower decks flooded. She heeled over and sank. Of the estimated seven hundred men on board, only around thirty were saved. Many were drowned by their heavy armour. Others could not escape because of the anti-boarding netting that covered the main deck.

The accident took place under the eyes of Henry VIII, who was watching the battle from Southsea castle with Lady Mary Carew, wife of Admiral Sir George Carew, who was on board the *Mary Rose*. His last words, shouted to his nephew Sir Gawen Carew, master of the *Matthew Gonson*, were, 'I have the sort of knaves I cannot rule.' So the crew, who drowned almost to a man, were to blame, then.

The French won the Battle of the Solent. They landed troops, but they made little headway. The following month they were taken off and, the following year, peace was declared.

Drake the rake

Sir Francis Drake is seen as the great seaman who saved England from the Spanish Armada. In fact, he put the realm in its greatest peril for the sake of money.

When the Armada was sighted in the Channel on 31 July 1588, Drake was famously playing bowls on Plymouth Hoe and insisted on finishing the game before finishing the Spanish. This story first appeared in a pamphlet in 1624, thirty-six years after the event. Later that day, Drake and the English fleet sailed. With clever manoeuvring, they got around behind the Spanish fleet – that is, to windward. The plan was to hold off from fighting until the Spanish intentions were clear. That night, Drake hauled a lantern up the main mast of his flagship, the *Revenge*, for the rest of the English fleet to follow. But suddenly the light went out.

Early that day, the flagship of the Andalusian squadron, the *Nuestra Señora del Rosario*, commanded by Don Pedro Valdés, had collided with the *Santa Catalina*, breaking her bowsprit and her main mast. She got left behind. Drake had a long career as a privateer before he sailed for the crown, and could not resist such a prize. He extinguished the lantern and went after the *Rosario*. When Drake caught up with her, Don Pedro found the *Rosario* alone against the man who had burned Cádiz. He put up no fight, surrendered and joined Drake for dinner in his cabin. The *Rosario* was carrying fifty thousand ducats to pay the Spanish army, along with over 600 tons of grapeshot and 2,300 rounds of heavy shot – ammunition for the rest of the fleet.

Without Drake's lantern to follow, the rest of the English fleet were thrown into disarray. The *Mary Rose*, the *White Bear* and the *Ark Royal*, carrying the commander-in-chief Lord Howard, mistook the lights of the Spanish ships for Drake and caught them up. Oar-powered Spanish galleasses under Hugo de Moncada turned to take them on. The loss of these three English ships would have proved disastrous for England, but the Spanish commander, Medina Sidonia, trying to keep his fleet together, called his galleys off. It was a lucky escape.

Drake took his prize into Torbay, loaded the gold onto the *Revenge* and rejoined the English fleet to see off the Spanish. Don Pedro Valdés was later ransomed, after spending much of his imprisonment in Drake's home. Much of the money on board the *Rosario* was thought to have been pocketed by Drake or Valdés, or both.

Other English captains did not take kindly to Drake's private enterprise. Martin Frobisher, another hero of the defeat of the Armada, accused Drake of making off with fifteen thousand ducats and threatened to 'spend the best blood of his belly' unless he hand over his share.

Dutch courage

The Dutch navy made an audacious raid on the Medway in 1667. They burned a number of ships and carried off as their prize the *Royal Charles*, the largest warship of the day, which destroyed their own flagship *Eendracht* during the Second Anglo-Dutch War. Her capture was the greatest humiliation in British naval history.

At the time, the British treasury was empty. The English Civil War had ended only sixteen years before. The Anglo-Dutch Wars had been dragging on intermittently since 1652. The plague had arrived in 1665 and London had burnt to the ground in 1666. There was no money to pay for fresh defences, or even pay the soldiers and sailors already on the rolls.

For two years Britain had been at war with the Dutch once again and the Lord Chancellor, the Earl of Clarendon, warned Charles II that he had two choices – either begin peace talks with the Dutch or make substantial concessions to Parliament. Unwilling to go cap in hand to the body that had chopped his father's head off, Charles began peace talks in Breda. Meanwhile, he pursued a third option. Under a secret pact, the French king Louis XIV would give him the money he desperately needed if he supported the French invasion of the Spanish Netherlands.

The Dutch knew that Charles was playing a double game and decided to take the ship that bore his name, which was moored at Chatham. Eighty Dutch ships turned up at the mouth of the Thames on 4 June. The king's secretary, Lord Arlington, dismissed this as mere bravado. The English did nothing, then panicked. The English man-of-war *Unity* fired one broadside before retreating up the Medway, and the inhabitants of Gravesend fled.

Two men were killed at the fort at Sheerness. The rest ran away. A chain across the mouth of the Medway was broken. As the Dutch sailed up the river they burnt four ships. The only resistance came not from the English but from the Scots on board the *Royal Oak*. Their captain, Archibald Douglas, perished in the fire on board and went down with the ship. Meanwhile, the Dutch seized the *Royal Charles* without opposition and sailed her down the Medway and back to Holland.

In London, people flocked to the banks to withdraw their money, fearing that the Dutch were on their way up the Thames to seize the capital. However, the Dutch only wanted to teach Charles a lesson. They signed the Treaty of Breda in 1667, ending the war.

The expression 'Dutch courage' comes from that era, but probably not from the calumny that the Dutch had to get drunk to attack England. Rather more commendably, it seems that Dutch sailors were the only ones courageous enough to sail up the Thames to deliver gin to London during the Great Plague.

Hang them

Admiral John Benbow had a proud record of taking on the French. He was in the Caribbean hunting Spanish treasure ships in 1702 when he heard of the outbreak of the War of the Spanish Succession, which gave him the opportunity to have a go at the old enemy again.

On 19 August, he spotted a French squadron under Admiral Jean du Casse in the Gulf of Venezuela. Although du Casse had nine ships and Benbow had only seven, he gave chase. He sent Captain Richard Kirby in HMS *Defiance* ahead to lead the line. But Kirby was slow and Benbow noticed that, when the *Defiance* and the *Windsor* under Captain John Constable came within range of the French, they quickly pulled back, even though their own men upbraided them for cowardice.

Benbow decided to take the lead in the *Breda*, but only the *Falmouth* and the smaller *Ruby* supported him. The other ships kept scrupulously out of harm's way. On the fifth day of the engagement, the *Ruby* was disabled and Benbow sent her back to Port Royal. The following day, Benbow's right leg was shattered by chain shot. Nevertheless, he stayed on deck to direct the fighting. The *Breda* disabled the seventy-gun *Apollon*. Though the *Defiance*, *Windsor*, *Greenwich* and *Pendennis* fired on the wreck, they would not come to Benbow's aid when du Casse bore down on the *Breda*. He even fired two shots at them to get them into line, to no avail, and du Casse made off with Benbow's prize.

Kirby came aboard the *Breda* to offer his commiserations over Benbow's injury. However, he said that the squadron was too weak to continue the fight, even though du Casse had already sent his slower ships off to safety in Cartagena. The other captains agreed with Kirby and all six signed a resolution to break off the engagement. Benbow had no alternative but to sail back to Port Royal.

There, his captains were arrested and he received a letter from du Casse that read:

Sir,

I had little hopes on Monday last but to have supped in your cabin: but it pleased God to order it otherwise. I am thankful for it. As for those cowardly captains who deserted you, hang them up, for by God they deserve it.

Yours,

du Casse

Captain Thomas Hudson of the *Pendennis* shot himself before the court martial, while Samuel Vincent, captain of the *Falmouth*, and Christopher Fogg, captain of the *Breda*, were initially sentenced to be cashiered for signing the captains' resolution, but Benbow personally declared that they had fought bravely and their sentences were remitted by the lord high admiral.

A lieutenant from the *Greenwich* told the court martial that Captain Cooper Wade was so afraid that he had said he was not prepared to defend himself if they were boarded. The lieutenant suggested, in that case, Wade go below and bolt the hatches, but Wade protested that the windows had not been boarded up and the French might use them to get in.

Kirby and Wade were sentenced to death. Constable was cashiered for drunkenness and neglect of duty. They were sent back to England as prisoners. Meanwhile, Benbow died of his wounds. Kirby and Wade were shot by a firing squad on board HMS *Bristol* in Plymouth Sound. Constable was incarcerated in the Marshalsea prison on the bank of the Thames, but pardoned by Queen Anne the following year.

Fog Bound

The Battle of Quebec in 1759 was one of the greatest victories in the history of the Empire. The attempt to take Quebec in 1711 was something entirely different.

Taking Quebec from the French was the idea of secretary of state and Tory grandee Henry St John, who picked his protégé Admiral Sir Hovenden Walker to command the expedition. To throw the French off the scent, he ordered that the fleet be loaded with three months' provision, as if it were sailing to the Mediterranean, rather than the eight months' worth needed for a transatlantic adventure. As the pubs of Plymouth, where the fleet assembled, were teeming with spies, it is unlikely that the French were fooled.

A further ruse was for two eighty-gun men-of-war to set off with the fleet, only to turn back – much to the surprise of Walker, who had not been in on the secret.

Landing in New England, short of food and money, Walker had more than five thousand soldiers and marines – as well as his crews – to feed. The cost of produce soared. Hungry seamen deserted and Walker had to press colonial fishermen into his crews to make up the numbers.

The next problem was to find a pilot to guide them up the St Lawrence. Most local pilots had been little further than the mouth of the river. The only one who had been further had sailed in a sloop and did not want to take responsibility for a man-of-war. Another contender was Colonel Samuel Vetch, a survivor of the Darien Scheme, Scotland's disastrous attempt to establish a colony in Central America. He had also been tried and convicted in a Massachusetts court of shipping guns to the French in Quebec. Although a soldier, he claimed to be the best pilot on the St Lawrence – a claim he later denied. Instead Walker picked a captured French sea captain named Paradis, who accepted a large bribe to guide them.

Once on the St Lawrence, they sailed into a thick fog and soon, due to the winds and currents, had little idea of where they were. On the night of 23 August 1711, Walker was getting ready for bed when he was told that breakers had been sighted. He assumed that he was too close to the south shore and ordered his ships to change tack. In fact, they were approaching the north shore and soon had breakers all around them. Summoned from his bed, Walker ordered his men-of-war to raise sail and stand off in the middle of the channel. But it was too late for some. Seven of the transports and one storeship ran aground. Out of a total of 1,390 military personnel, 705 soldiers and 35 women attached to the regiments, along with around 150 sailors, were either drowned or died from exposure on shore.

Walker cruised up and down the shore for two days trying to save what men and stores he could. Following a council of war, it was decided that they had no choice but to abandon the expedition. More bad luck befell Walker. Back in England, his flagship *Edgar* blew up with the loss of his entire crew and his logs, charts and journals. Walker was in London at the time, where his reception was not as hostile as he had expected. However, soon after, the Tories fell from power and the Whigs called for a full enquiry. Unable to defend himself without his paperwork, Walker was dismissed.

Admiral Hosier's Ghost

In 1726, Vice-Admiral Francis Hosier was sent to the Caribbean to prevent Spanish treasure ships sailing from Porto Bello. He succeeded. But unlike Henry Morgan, who plundered the city in 1668, he was not a pirate. And unlike Admiral Edward Vernon, who seized the port in 1739, he did not have the excuse of England's being at war with Spain, so he could not attack the city.

Realising the constraints on Hosier, the Spaniards did not send out their treasure ships. They unloaded them and sent the treasure back to Panama, leaving the ships riding provocatively at anchor. Consequently, to fulfil his mission, Hosier had to remain on station, blockading the port. His sailors began to ail with 'yellow jack' or 'black vomit' – yellow fever. So many died that Hosier had to sail to Jamaica to recruit more. They died too. Four thousand men died, including some fifty lieutenants, and eight or ten captains and flag officers and Hosier himself. He was embalmed and his body was returned to England on the sloop *Happy*.

After the success of Vernon's attack on Porto Bello, Richard Glover wrote the poem 'Admiral Hosier's Ghost':

> Heed, Oh heed, our fatal story –
> I am Hosier's injur'd ghost –
> You, who have now purchased glory
> At this place where I was lost,
> Though in Portobello's ruin
> You now triumph, free from fears,
> When you think on our undoing,
> You will mix your joy with tears! . . .
>
> See these mournful spectres sweeping,
> Ghastly o'er this hated wave,
> Whose wan cheeks are stained with weeping:
> These were English captains brave.
> Mark those numbers pale and horrid –,
> Who were once my sailors bold,
> Lo, each hangs his drooping forehead,
> While his dismal tale is told . . .
>
> . . . Unrepining at thy glory,
> Thy successful arms we hail;
> But remember our sad story,
> And let Hosier's wrongs prevail

Sent in this foul clime to languish,
Think what thousands fell in vain,
Not in glorious battle slain . . .

. . . After this proud foe subduing,
When your patriot friends you see,
Think on vengeance for my ruin,
And for England shamed in me.

The poem shifted the blame for the fate of Hosier's expedition on prime minister Sir Robert Walpole, who had sent him. Walpole fell from power soon after it was published.

Cashiered for fighting

Admiral Thomas Mathews and Vice-Admiral Richard Lestock did not get on. During their long and distinguished careers, they had frequently butted up against each other. The last straw came when Mathews was appointed commander of the Mediterranean Fleet over Lestock's head. Tempers were made no better by the fact that Mathews suffered from a painful urinary condition, known then as 'the gravel', while Lestock had gout.

On 8 February 1744, a Franco-Spanish fleet sailed out of Toulon. The British fleet was moored just twenty miles down the coast at Villefranche. Lestock went aboard Mathews's flagship, the *Namur*, and asked what his orders were. Mathews said he had no orders and bid Lestock a curt goodnight.

The following day, when they went into action, Lestock

commanded the rear. As the *Namur* plunged into the centre of the action, Lestock held back. His excuse was that he was just obeying orders. Mathews had not struck the line-in-battle signal, so he was not, technically, permitted to break ranks and engage the enemy on his own initiative. The rest of the British fleet suffered a severe mauling and was forced to flee to Minorca, where Lestock was dismissed.

Back in London, Mathews and Lestock then fought a battle every bit as bitter as the Battle of Toulon. They slugged it out in pamphlets and in Parliament. The public favoured Mathews, but Lestock was well connected politically and got the better of it in the official inquiry. Courts martial followed. However, they were fixed in Lestock's favour. He was exonerated, made a full admiral and given command of an expedition to North America. Mathews was cashiered. However, a naval historian writing in 1758 said that 'the nation could not be persuaded that the vice-admiral ought to be exculpated for not fighting and the admiral cashiered for fighting'.

Drunk on duty

Captain Thomas Watson, who had served under Admiral Vernon at Cartagena, had fractured his skull. As a result, even the smallest swig of alcohol rendered him roaring drunk. However, there were difficulties obtaining a medical diagnosis of his condition, especially while he was at sea.

On 8 May 1744, he was in command of the seventy-gun *Northumberland* off the coast of Ushant when he was ordered to pursue an unidentified vessel by Vice-Admiral

Charles Hardy. As the weather grew stormy, Hardy signalled for Watson to return. But Watson continued his pursuit, even though two more ships turned up. They were French. A Royal Navy ship of the line should still have had the advantage. But Watson went into battle without even having cleared the men's hammocks from the gun decks. He refused to call for help from the fleet and, instead of picking the French ships off one at a time, he attacked all of them at once.

Watson was killed by a cannonball. None of the lieutenants were prepared to take over, so command passed to the master, Dixon. He promptly surrendered. Renamed the *Atlas*, the *Northumberland* remained on the French navy lists for fifty years.

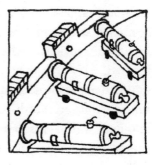

While Watson, who was said to be drunk, was blamed for the loss of the *Northumberland*, Dixon was sentenced to life in Marshalsea Prison for surrendering a ship of the line.

Pour encourager les autres

The French author Voltaire said in his book *Candide* that the English find it necessary to shoot an admiral from time to time '*pour encourager les autres*' – 'to encourage the others'. The man he had in mind was Admiral John Byng.

In February 1756, immediately before the outbreak of the Seven Years' War between Britain and France, it became clear that the French aimed to take the British-held island of Minorca. A fleet of twelve battleships under Admiral de la Galissonière had been assembled at Toulon, ready to escort the Duc de Richelieu and an army of sixteen thousand men to the island. So a British fleet was hastily assembled under Admiral Byng.

While Byng was the highest-ranking officer in the navy except for the First Sea Lord, his rise through the ranks was due to patronage. His father had been an admiral and he became a captain at the age of twenty-three; a rear admiral at forty-one. But he had no experience of action and had spent the previous fifteen years in comfortable postings on land.

Eight of the ships he was given were unfit for action. The other four were seriously undermanned. When Byng arrived at Gibraltar, the governor gave him only minimal help for fear of weakening the defences there. He even withheld the troops that Byng was supposed to transport to Minorca. They were to be held in reserve to see off any French attack on Gibraltar.

When Byng arrived off Minorca, he saw, much to his relief, that the Union Flag was still flying above St Philip's Castle, where the eighty-two-year-old General Blakeney and two thousand men were holding out. With no troops to land, Byng engaged the French Navy. But his ramshackle fleet was easily outclassed by the French ships. With no experience of war, Byng tried to follow the Admiralty's Fighting Instructions, which had been written in the late seventeenth century and were hopelessly out of date. His captains had trouble following the arcane signals he gave. He failed to seize the opportunity to get between the French fleet and the island, denying them the harbour, or to cut their supply lines to Toulon.

After proving himself incompetent – though not cowardly – he called a council of war. His captains agreed that they had no real prospect of relieving Minorca and he decided to withdraw to Gibraltar. Abandoned, Blakeney duly surrendered after seventy days of siege.

A scapegoat was needed. Byng was the obvious choice. The prime minister, Lord Newcastle, promised that 'he shall be tried immediately; he shall be hanged directly'. Byng was court-martialled and found guilty of failing to do 'his utmost to take, seize and destroy the ships of the French king'. However, the admirals in the court asked that the death penalty be set aside. William Pitt argued for clemency, and both Voltaire and Richelieu sent petitions from France – though it cannot have done Byng much good to have the enemy on his side.

Byng was executed by firing squad on the foredeck of HMS *Monarch* – a ship he had once commanded – on 14 March 1757. Everyone knew that Newcastle was really to blame for the incompetent handling of affairs at a time of national crisis. He fell from power. However, he remained minister of finance in Pitt's administration for the next five years.

The other Armada

During the American War of Independence, with the British otherwise occupied, the French saw an opportunity to invade England. In 1779, they assembled two armies of twenty thousand men with their transports at Le Havre and St Malo. The plan was for the French fleet under the Comte d'Orvilliers to rendezvous with the Spanish fleet at Corunna. They would then drive the Royal Navy out of the Channel, allowing the troops to land at Portsmouth and march on London.

But things did not go according to plan. The French government was short of money and could not pay its sailors properly. Men were recruited from hospitals and prisons. Ordinary seamen were made officers and, on some ships, not even the captain knew how to take a bearing. Making up the numbers delayed the sailing from May to early June.

When the French arrived at Corunna, the seventy-three-year-old Admiral Don Luis de Córdova expressed surprise. He said he did not know they were coming and it took another six weeks for him to get ready. As it was, the Spaniards were not happy about obeying French orders and tried to dissuade d'Orvilliers from invading England, urging him to attack Gibraltar instead. But d'Orvilliers was determined to go ahead and inflict the greatest possible humiliation on his country's proud rival.

As it set off for the Channel, the Franco-Spanish Armada comprised sixty-six ships-of-the-line and numerous frigates and smaller vessels. The most the British could hope to put to sea were forty. The Royal Navy was also in disarray. After failing to win a decisive victory over d'Orvilliers at Ushant in 1778, the commander Admiral Augustus Keppel fell out with his deputy Admiral Hugh Palliser, who was backed by the first lord of the Admiralty, John Montagu, Earl of Sandwich. The contending parties were known, flippantly, as the Montagus and the Keppulets.

Keppel resigned as commander of the Channel Fleet in March 1779. Out of hatred of Sandwich, Keppel's friends Lord Howe and Lord Mann refused to take the job. Instead, Sandwich appointed Vice-Admiral Sir Charles Hardy, the governor of Greenwich Hospital, who had not been to sea for fifteen years – hardly an inspired choice.

Even as the Franco-Spanish Armada left Corunna, the French ships were running low on provisions because of the repeated delays. Soon the sailors were coming down with scurvy. This was followed by smallpox and 'putrid fever'. D'Orvillier's son died in his arms, which seemed to knock the stuffing out of him. Plaintively, d'Orvilliers wrote to the French government, begging for more men and provisions. None were forthcoming.

As the fleet entered the Channel, they encountered the August gales. Somehow they reached Plymouth, only to be blown back out again into the Atlantic. The plan to make a landing at Portsmouth was abandoned. Instead they would take Plymouth. The French would then over-winter in Cornwall before marching on London. But, after d'Orvilliers had battled his way back to Plymouth, the Armada was blown out into the Atlantic once more. The best he could do was to lie off the Scilly Isles and hope to ambush the British fleet if it sailed by.

Hardy set sail with great words about the defeat of the Armada in 1588 ringing in his ears. Inspired by Drake, Hawkins and Frobisher, he was to take on the new Armada. But he could not find it. By the time he reached the Scilly Isles, d'Orvilliers was back at Plymouth once more. When the two fleets did catch sight of each other, Hardy retreated to Spithead, ostensibly aiming to lure the French into the confined waters there. But d'Orvilliers had lost heart and returned to France, where he resigned his command and withdrew to a seminary.

Hardy was criticised for his withdrawal. Had he attacked d'Orvilliers's battered and dispirited Armada like Drake – or Nelson – he would have scored a tremendous victory. But he successfully defended his conduct before Parliament and on 17 May 1780 hoisted his admiral's flag on the *Victory*. He died two days later from a seizure caused by an inflammation of the bowel.

That sinking feeling

In 1782, England was at war with Spain again and, that August, a fleet was being assembled at Spithead when the flagship *Royal George* unexpectedly sank. The ship was hosting a 'wedding garland' at the time, when 'wives' could visit their husbands on board before they went into action – as shore leave was cancelled due to the danger of desertion.

The ship was heeled over to repair a pump. A lighter – a flat-bottomed barge used for transferring goods – seized the opportunity to load extra casks of rum through the lower gunports near the waterline on the other side, rather than haul them up over the rail. This extra weight tipped the ship a little further until seawater began splashing through the gunports. The carpenter went to warn the lieutenant of the watch that they were about to sink. He took no notice, but the carpenter was insistent. However, by the time he had ordered the drummer to beat the order 'Right Ship', water was pouring through the gunports and the *Royal George* capsized.

More than 400 crewmen and 360 women and children were drowned, along with Admiral Richard Kempenfelt, said to be the cleverest man in the navy. A court martial found no one to blame, concluding that there had been a structural failure of the ship's 'old and rotten' frame – though this had never been mentioned before.

Chinese junk

In 1808, Rear Admiral William O'Bryen Drury was sent with two frigates and transports carrying a thousand soldiers and marines to prevent the French occupying the Portuguese colony of Macao. Once Macao had been taken, the East India Company urged him to sail up the Pearl River to protect Britain's tea trade at Canton.

Drury was dubious about this enterprise, fearing a full-scale confrontation with the Chinese. What was required was a bit of a show. He led the flotilla from his admiral's barge, hoping to establish cordial relations with the Chinese commander. However, local peasants who knew nothing

221

of the might of the Royal Navy flocked to the riverbanks and began throwing rotten vegetables, fruit and offal at the foreign devils. One peasant woman threw a stone that hit a British sailor on the head and drew blood.

Now Drury had a choice. He could either fire on the peasants on the banks and show them who was boss, or avoid a massacre and withdraw. He withdraw. The Chinese emperor then ordered Drury to withdraw from Macao, as he had leased it to the Portuguese, not the British.

Drury's bad luck continued. In 1810, he led an invasion of Mauritius, at that time a French possession. However, when the invasion was almost complete, Rear Admiral Albemarle Bertie, who outranked him, turned up and stole the credit. Drury complained to the Admiralty, but died soon after.

Suicide mission

The Crimean War, curiously, was not confined to the Crimea. French and English fleets attacked Russian shipping wherever they could. In 1854, Rear Admiral David Price, who had been shore-bound, mostly on half pay, for forty years, was made commander-in-chief in the Pacific. That August, he was with a squadron pursuing two Russian frigates that took refuge in Petropavlovsk on the Kamchatka peninsula. However, the port was well defended with the Russian warship *Aurora* hidden behind a sandbank in a position where it could deliver a broadside to anyone entering.

Unable to bear the responsibility of commanding men in action, Price shot himself. But he could not even do this properly. Instead of hitting the heart, the bullet lodged painfully in his lungs. Despite the pain, he apologised to fellow officers and the chaplain for his 'crime'.

After Price was duly buried on shore, the attack on Petropavlovsk went ahead. It was decisively repelled with more than two hundred casualties, and the Royal Navy withdrew.

Crimean crimes

In March 1854, the secretary of state for war, another Lord Newcastle, sent orders to the Admiralty, telling the commander of the Baltic Fleet, Admiral Sir Charles 'Mad Charley' Napier, 'to respect private property . . . and on no account to attack defenceless places and open towns'. However, this seems to have had no effect on Rear Admiral James Plumridge, commander of a squadron of paddle steamers, and Captain Gifford of HMS *Leopard*, who took a singular delight in attacking Finnish ports. They destroyed forty-six vessels; 40,000–50,000 barrels of pitch and tar; 6,000 square yards of rough pitch; stacks of timber, spars, planks and deal; and sails, rope and various kinds of naval stores. The total value of the goods at that time amounted to £300,000 to £400,000. Much of this material was actually British property, already paid for and awaiting export. Even Napier seemed pleased – until London trading houses began complaining and *The Times* condemned attacks on friendly trading partners.

The attacks stirred up anti-British sentiment in neutral Sweden and forced even the Anglophile Finns to seek the protection of the tsar. Russian troops were sent and fifty-two crew members of the paddle steamer *Vulture* were killed in a raid on Gamlakarleby. More battles ensued. To defend Finland, an electric telegraph link was set up between St Petersburg and Helsinki and the northern towns. Then a railway was built. This paved the way for Finland's independence in 1917.

Wrong turn

Vice-Admiral Sir George Tryon had a long and distinguished naval career. In 1861, he had been given command of Britain's first seagoing iron-clad. He was tall, broad and bearded, and did not like being gainsaid.

By 1889, he was commanding the Mediterranean Fleet, and on 22 June 1893 a little after 2 p.m. the fleet was off Tripoli. The ships were formed in two columns, twelve hundred yards apart. About half past three, the order was given to invert the course in succession, turning inwards to come about to anchor. This caused consternation in the ranks. The turning circle of the capital ships was sixteen hundred yards. There would not be enough room to manoeuvre. No one dared take this up with Tryon. Then one brave junior spoke up. Tryon grudgingly amended the order, but then returned to the original one.

Tryon's flagship, HMS *Victoria*, which was only three months old, was at the head of one rank, while the *Camperdown*, under his second-in-command, Rear Admiral Albert Hastings Markham, led the other one. Markham knew that the manoeuvre was suicidal, but did as he was ordered anyway. As the ships came about, Tryon saw that the *Victoria* and the *Camperdown* were bound to collide. Anticipating the disaster, the *Victoria*'s commander, Captain Archibald Bourke, asked whether they should do something. Tryon seemed mesmerised. Eventually, Bourke became insistent.

'May I go astern?' he said.

Tryon whispered, 'Yes, go astern.'

But it was too late. The twin screws of the *Victoria* were thrown into reverse, but the *Camperdown* received no such order until they were within hailing distance. She rammed into the side of the *Victoria*, her pointed bow ripping a huge hole in the starboard. Other ships lowered their boats, but Tryon countermanded that, considering that his flagship had not been hit in a vital spot. However, the ship had been designed with a low forecastle. She flooded rapidly, turned over and went down in a flat calm.

Tryon went down with his ship. One of the few to survive was John Jellicoe, who was in the sick bay and escaped in his pyjamas. He went on to command the Grand Fleet during the First World War.

Markham sailed into port with a band playing on the quarterdeck, which was considered to be in bad taste. Nevertheless, he was exonerated by a court martial – held conveniently out of the way in Malta – though it was regretted that he did not question the order he had been given. But, as the Duke of Cambridge commented, 'It is better to go wrong according to orders that to go wrong in opposition to orders.'

South Sea bubbles

In 1889, while a civil war was going on in Samoa, there was a confrontation between Germany, the United States and Great Britain there. In all, seven of the great powers' warships were crammed into the small harbour of Apia. The Germans were represented by the *Olga*, the *Eber* and the *Alder*; the US by the *Trenton*, the *Nipsic* and the *Vandalia*. The British had just one cruiser, HMS *Calliope*, on hand.

Ignoring warnings that a typhoon was on its way, the Americans refused to leave. The Germans stayed because the Americans were there. But the *Calliope* made for the high sea. When the typhoon hit, the *Olga* was tossed ashore, while the *Eber* and the *Alder* were smashed into each other and sank with a loss of ninety-six lives. The USS *Vandalia* went down with a loss of a hundred men; the *Trenton* and the *Nipsic* ran aground with light casualties.

Meanwhile, making just one knot against 100mph winds, the *Calliope* made it out into open water and survived undamaged.

Shipshape and Bristol fashion

For a century after Trafalgar, the Royal Navy rarely had to go into battle. All it had to do was turn up in foreign ports and show the flag. So it was all-important for national prestige for the men to be turned out well and the ships to be clean and tidy.

Watertight doors were polished so often that they were shiny, but no longer watertight. The guns were purely decorative and gunnery drills were rare, as smoke from the practice shells dirtied the paintwork. All this would be changed by a young gunnery officer named Percy Scott. He was serving with the Mediterranean Fleet in 1882 when it bombarded Alexandria. Of the three thousand shells fired, only ten hit the forts the Egyptians were building there. Still, it took until 1903 before gunnery practice was added to the annual inspection of a ship of the line.

Even then, the shells supplied to the navy were largely duds. They were supplied with faulty fuses and only half filled with gunpowder. And his suggestions for improvements to the accuracy of gun sights fell on deaf ears at the Admiralty. However, foreign navies were interested and he began to earn money from his patents.

In 1905, Scott was promoted rear admiral and made inspector of target practice, a post created for him. He found that every gun sight in the fleet was inaccurate.

The problem was not just with the sights and the men's paucity of training: it was with the design of the ships themselves. Smoke from the forward turrets obscured the vision of the rear turrets, so no forward firing was allowed. To cure the problem, a mast carrying an observation platform was added to HMS *Dreadnought*, launched in 1906. However, it was sited behind the funnel, so the observer was both smoked and roasted. On one occasion, the mast became so hot that the observer had to stay up it for several days while food and water were hauled up to him.

Scott suggested that the observation platforms should be moved in front of the funnel, but the Admiralty continued to insist that they looked better behind the funnel until 1912. Even then, the new mast was too flimsy to carry the weight of the observer and gunnery practice took place only on clear days and into the wind. Poor gunnery continued to dog the fleet throughout the

First World War. Even in the Second World War, HMS *King George V* and the *Rodney* fired 719 shells at *Bismarck* without hitting her, even when her steering gear was put out of action. She had to be finished off with torpedoes.

Live bait

On 21 August 1914, Commodore Roger Keyes, commanding the submarine squadron at Harwich, wrote to his superior, Admiral Sir Arthur Leveson, urging that *Bacchante*-class cruisers patrolling the North Sea be withdrawn from service. Fourteen years old, they were unsuited to modern warfare and vulnerable to attack by submarine, so much so that they were known in the Navy as the 'live-bait squadron'. His concern was passed up the chain of command and, on 18 September, the first lord of the Admiralty, Winston Churchill, wrote a memo, saying, 'The *Bacchantes* ought not to continue on this beat. The risks to such ships is not justified by any services they can render.'

Nevertheless three *Bacchante*-class cruisers – *Aboukir*, *Hogue* and *Cressy* – remained on patrol in the 'Broad

Fourteens', the northern approaches to the English Channel where the depth is uniformly fourteen fathoms. This was an area known for submarine attacks. The *Bacchante* herself was in dock undergoing repairs. Rear Admiral Arthur Christian, who should have been leading the patrol, was also in dock with his flagship *Euryalus*. The cruisers' destroyer escort had been withdrawn due to bad weather. Due to shortages of manpower, their officers were from the Royal Naval Reserve, rather than regular sailors, and the crews were brought up to strength by four hundred fifteen- and sixteen-year-olds from the Royal Naval College, Dartmouth. Live bait indeed.

At 6 a.m. on 22 September, Lieutenant Otto Weddigen, commander of the German submarine U-9, spotted the three cruisers. They were not zigzagging, but steaming calmly in a line abreast at just ten knots to conserve coal. At 6.20 a.m., he fired a torpedo, which struck the *Aboukir* on the starboard side. The engine room flooded, causing the ship to stop immediately. As no submarine had been sighted, her commander, Captain John Drummond, assumed that she had hit a mine and summoned help from the other two cruisers.

Meanwhile, he ordered the boats be lowered, only to discover that most of them had been left behind at Chatham to save weight. With the ship listing at twenty degrees, some could not be lowered, which flooded the engine room and put the steam-driven derrick that lowered the pinnace (a small boat) out of order. There were not even enough boats to accommodate a quarter of the men.

The *Hogue* drew alongside to take the men off. She now

presented Lieutenant Weddigen with a stationary target. Two torpedoes hit the *Hogue*. Her magazine exploded and she sank. Meanwhile, the *Aboukir* turned turtle and went down as well.

Realising that there was a submarine in the vicinity, the *Cressy* began firing at driftwood – in the mistaken belief that it was a periscope. She also fired on an innocent Dutch trawler, thought to be a spotter for the German attack.

There were eighteen hundred men in the water. The *Cressy* had no choice but to come to a halt and drop nets over the side. Weddigen was presented with another stationary target. Two more torpedoes sank the third cruiser.

Later, British trawlers and Dutch steamships rescued 837 men, while 1,459 perished. The three captains were publicly pilloried – Churchill wanted them court-martialled – but, as usual, those high up in the Admiralty responsible for the outdated craft going to sea in the first place got off scot-free.

The Battle of May Island

At the beginning of the First World War, German U-boat technology was streets ahead of its British counterpart, as the use of submarines was considered sneaky, underhand and un-English. Even Churchill, as first lord of the Admiralty, said that no civilised nation would resort to such tactics. Nevertheless, fire must be fought with fire and in 1915 fourteen K-class submarines were commissioned. They would prove to be more of a danger to themselves and other British shipping than they were to the enemy.

The Sea Lords wanted a submarine with a top speed of twenty-four knots so it could keep up with the huge dreadnought-type battleships. Commodore Roger Keyes, who had commanded the small E-class submarines at the Battle of Heligoland Bight in 1914, pointed out that it was a mistake to deploy submarines along with surface ships. Due to the impracticality of communication with them, the submarines proved only to be a distraction. During the battle, three Royal Navy cruisers had tried to run down the British submarines, mistaking them for U-boats. He was overruled.

The speed was to be provided by two steam turbines. This meant that the coal fires heating the boilers would have to be extinguished and their funnels sealed when the submarine submerged. So the K-class submarine would take at least five minutes to dive, while a diesel-powered U-boat could be underwater in thirty seconds. And when the British sub surfaced it would be a sitting duck until the fires were started again.

The K-class submarine was also equipped with two periscopes and a retractable radio mast, along with other vents, hatches, guns and torpedo tubes. The hull was full of holes, any one of which could spring a leak. Construction went ahead anyway.

The new submarine would be three times the size of an E-class sub and have the displacement of a destroyer. It would be 339ft (103m) long. That meant that, at an angle of thirty degrees, the stern would be out of the water, while the bow would be nearing its maximum designed diving depth of 200ft (60m). In fact, in trials, its maximum safe depth was only 70ft (20m), which meant it could operate only at an angle of around ten degrees. Little wonder that the K-class submarine became known at the 'Kalamity class'. Such scuttlebutt meant little to the Admiralty, who commissioned seven more before the first had even undergone sea trials.

K3 was the first to be completed. Conditions in the boiler room proved to be impossibly hot and, even on the surface, water often splashed in through the funnels, extinguishing the coal fires heating the boilers. A heavy sea broke the window of the wheelhouse and a British patrol boat fired on her. In December 1916, with the Duke of York and future King George VI on board, she nose-dived, burying her bows in the mud at the bottom of Stokes Bay while her stern stuck out above the waves. It took twenty minutes to free her. On 9 January 1917, K3's boiler room was flooded in the North Sea.

On 19 January, during a test dive in Gare Loch. K13's rear compartment flooded, drowning thirty-two men. Another forty-eight were trapped. But they were in only sixty feet (18 metres) of water, which meant that rescue was possible. Commander Francis Goodhart, captain of K14, who was on board as an observer, tried to go for help, but he hit his head on his way out of the submarine and drowned. However, Lieutenant-Commander Godfrey Herbert made it to the surface alive and got help. Another submarine, E51, attached a high-pressure line and blew K13's ballast tank. The bow then appeared above the surface. A hole was cut in the hull and, after fifty-four hours, the remaining forty-six men were rescued. K13 was then raised, refitted and recommissioned as K22.

Every one of the thirteen K-class submarines to be tested between January and May 1917 showed a major fault. K6, for example, sank and remained on the bottom until her compressed-air system was fixed. K4 ran aground on Waley Island. When K2 caught fire, it was found that there were no fire extinguishers on board. A bucket chain of sailors had to be set up to dowse the fire with seawater. K14 also suffered an electrical fire. Nevertheless, they were sent to join the fleet in Scapa Flow.

In June, five of them were sent with a flotilla of destroyers to perform an anti-submarine sweep of the North Sea. Under their eyes, nine British merchant ships were sunk by U-boats. K7 was mistaken for a U-boat and depth-charged by two Royal Navy destroyers, but escaped. She then spotted a U-boat and fired a torpedo, which hit the German craft amidships but did not explode. A second torpedo missed. After loosing off a few shots, the U-boat made a rapid dive. K7 was unable to follow her.

K1 ran aground, but the captain was excused on the grounds that rats had eaten part of his sea charts. That November, K1 collided with K4 off the Danish coast and had to be scuttled to avoid capture.

Then, in January 1918, a major catastrophe occurred. Two flotillas of K-class submarines were heading down the Firth of Forth with a battle fleet of cruisers and their destroyer escorts. The night was clear and the sea was calm. To elude German U-boats thought to be operating in the area, each showed only a dim stern light. Off May Island, K14's helm jammed. She cut her engines to avoid going round in circles and was run into by K22 – the recommissioned K13. K14 was crippled and sinking and, as K22 called for help, she was hit by the battle cruiser HMS *Inflexible*, bending her bows at right angles. She settled by the bow with only her conning tower showing above water.

The rest of the fleet turned back to help. The cruiser HMS *Fearless* collided with K17. She sank in about eight minutes, though most of the crew escaped, only to be run down in the water by the ships following. While the submarines behind turned to avoid her, K6 hit K4, nearly cutting her in half. She was then struck by K7 and sank with all her crew.

In just seventy-five minutes, two submarines had been sunk, four badly damaged – along with one cruiser – and 105 crew killed. No enemy had been sighted. The incident became known as the Battle of May Island and was kept secret under wartime restrictions. A committee of enquiry concluded that submarines could not work safely with surface craft – something Commodore Keyes had known in 1914. Nevertheless, more K-class submarines were commissioned and more sank with no sign of the enemy.

On 2 May 1918, K3 dived uncontrollably to 266 feet, which crushed part of the hull. On 20 January 1921, K5 sank with all hands during a mock battle in the Bay of Biscay. On 25 June, K15 sank at her moorings in Portsmouth. The rest were scrapped. None were lost due to enemy action.

Advance and be recognised

On 12 March 1916, the Royal Navy submarine D3 was on patrol in the Channel when she was spotted on the surface by a French airship. Seeing a friendly craft, the crew of the submarine fired rockets as a recognition signal. The French interpreted this as hostile fire and bombed D3. Some of the submariners got out. Hearing their cries in English, the airship summoned help, but the men had drowned before it arrived.

Getting the sums right

During the early months of 1917, Britain's shipping losses to U-boats soared to the point that the country was on the verge of surrender. But, when it was suggested that a convoy system should be introduced, the aptly named Rear Admiral Duff, head of the Anti-Submarine Division, opposed the idea, claiming that weekly shipping losses amounted to a tiny percentage of the five thousand vessels that sailed every week. Providing a submarine screen for so many ships would prove impossible.

However, when Duff's figures were checked they were proved to be utterly wrong. Discounting the movements of trawlers, ferries, coasters and local traffic, only 130 merchant ships put to sea each week, a number well within the Royal Navy's capacity to escort. What's more, some forty losses a week represent nearly a third of all those who sailed. While 155 ships were sunk in April 1917, in August when the convoy system was introduced, only five of the eight hundred ships on the high seas were sunk.

U or non-U?

As part of the battle against German U-boats in the First World War, the British employed Q-ships – merchantmen with concealed guns. One of them was the *Cymric*, a sailing ship fitted with a twin-screw engine, a four-inch gun and two twelve-pounders.

On 15 October 1918, she was patrolling off the coast of Yorkshire, when she nearly fired on a K-class submarine, further damaging their score. The next time, the *Cymric*'s crew were called to action stations, they were disappointed to discover that their intended prey was, again, a friendly vessel.

Then they thought they had struck lucky. They saw what they took to be a U-boat with the ident 'U-6' clearly inscribed on the conning tower, dropped their camouflage and fired. The ident painted on the conning tower was, in fact, 'J-6', but something hanging over the side provided a second upright on the 'J'. It was only when they were fishing survivors out of the water that their mistake was recognised.

Own goal

In March 1942, HMS *Trinidad* was escorting Arctic convoy PQ13 around Norway to the White Sea and

Russia. It was so cold that the sea spray froze as soon as it hit the deck. Three German destroyers closed in and there was an exchange of fire. Then the *Trinidad* fired three torpedoes. Two were so badly frozen that they stuck in the tubes. The third was fired, but its gyroscope was frozen and it circled around and hit the *Trinidad* amidships. Though badly damaged, she managed to limp into Murmansk.

CHAPTER TEN

Aerial Engagements

W HEN WAR TOOK TO THE air, fighter pilots heralded a new age of chivalry in which battles would be decided in single combat. However, the new age of chivalry was just as prone to pomposity and braggadocio as the old. And some of the equipment was as ludicrous as the loricas, hauberks, plastrons and habergeons of earlier times.

The 'pulpit'

During the First World War, some 3,500 Royal Aircraft Factory BE2 biplanes were built – the BE stood for Blériot Experimental. But they soon became vulnerable to German fighters. German pilots called it *Kaltes Fleish* – 'Cold Meat' – while the British press dubbed the BE2 'Fokker Fodder'.

To improve its defences, a streamlined plywood compartment or nacelle, popularly known as the 'pulpit', was added in front of the propeller. This accommodated an airman with a Lewis gun on a flexible mount, giving

THE BEASTLY BATTLES OF OLD ENGLAND

the plane a forward field of fire in the days before the development of interrupter gears that synchronised the gun and propeller.

However, the gunner was in danger of being sucked into the propeller and sliced to pieces, or crushed by the engine in the gentlest of crashes. A prototype went into action in France. It proved unpopular and the plane did not go into mass production.

Bloody silly name

The Spitfire is now remembered as the plane that won the Battle of Britain. But the directors of Supermarine, the original manufacturers of the plane, wanted to call it the Shrike or the Shrew. The name Spitfire was suggested by Sir Robert Maclean, director of the parent company Vickers-Armstrong, who called his daughter Ann 'the little spitfire'. The word actually originated in the seventeenth century and originally meant that which 'spits fire' – a cannon or a hot-tempered creature. When the designer Reginald Mitchell heard what the company was going to call his plane, he said, 'Just the sort of bloody silly name they would choose.'

The first of the few

The first Spitfire to appear in public in RAF colours took to the air on Empire Air Day, 20 May 1939, during a display at Duxford. However, the pilot forgot to lower his undercarriage and 'belly-landed' his plane. He was fined £5. Others also found it hard to get the hang of. By the outbreak of the Second World War on 3 September, thirty-six had already been written off in accidents.

The Battle of Barking Creek

The first encounter of the Battle of Britain pitted the RAF against the RAF over the Medway and ended with a tragic own goal. At 6.15 a.m. on 6 September 1939, with the war just three days old, the newly installed radar system malfunctioned and reported unidentified aircraft approaching at high altitude over West Mersea on the Essex Coast. The Hurricanes of 56 and 151 Squadron, based at North Weal Barking Creek, were scrambled. So were the Spitfires of 54, 63 and 74 Squadron from Hornchurch.

Over Essex, 'A' flight of 74 Squadron reported seeing what they took to be enemy planes. None of them had been in combat before, nor had they seen a German aircraft. They were give permission to engage them. Zeroing in on what were, in fact, two straggling Hurricanes, Flying Officer Paddy Byrne and Pilot Officer John Freeborn opened fire.

One Hurricane was piloted by Frank Rose, who survived. The other was flown by Pilot Officer Montague Hulton-Harrop, who was shot in the back of the head and was dead before he hit the ground – the first British casualty of the Second World War. Meanwhile, anti-aircraft fire downed a Blenheim.

It was later discovered that the air-raid warning had been a false alarm. The pilots were exonerated by a court martial, though Group Captain Lucking was removed from his post as commanding officer of 56 Squadron. The leader of 'A' flight, Adolph 'Sailor' Malan, went on to lead 74 Squadron at the height of the Battle of Britain, scoring twenty-seven kills, seven shared destroyed, three probably destroyed and sixteen damaged. John Freeborn, the pilot who had actually downed Hulton-Harrop's plane, also survived the war. During the Battle of Britain he was awarded the Distinguished Flying Cross and bar. He rose to become a wing commander and was credited with seventeen kills.

'You British are mad'

The Fairey Battle light bomber was the first plane in service with the RAF with the Rolls-Royce Merlin engine that would power the Hurricane, Spitfire, Lancaster and Wellington bomber. On 20 September 1939, a German Messerschmitt Bf 109 was shot down by Battle gunner Sergeant F. Letchard during a patrol near Aachen, giving the RAF its first aerial victory of the war.

However, the Battle was hopelessly outdated. It was almost a hundred miles an hour slower than a Bf 109 at fourteen thousand feet. It had a single .303 Vickers K machine gun mounted in the rear cockpit and a single forward-firing Browning machine gun in the starboard wing. And as a low-level bomber it was extremely vulnerable to light anti-aircraft fire.

On 10 May 1940, thirteen out of thirty-two Battles airborne were lost. The following day, seven out of eight sent up by the RAF were lost, while the Belgian Air Force lost another six. On the 12th, five Battles attacked bridges across the River Meuse. Four were shot down; the other crashed returning to base. One of the pilots escaped and parachuted to earth behind enemy lines. The German officer who captured him said, 'You British are mad. You give us all Friday and Saturday to get our flak guns up in circles all around the bridge, and then on Sunday, when all is ready, you come along with three aircraft and try to blow the thing up.'

Two days later thirty-five out of the sixty-three Battles airborne were lost, along with five out of the eight Bristol Blenheims. In mid-June the Battles were withdrawn. By then, two hundred had been lost.

The flying coffin

In December 1940, Air Chief Marshal Robert Brooke-Popham, commander-in-chief of the British Far East Command, was reviewing the defences of Singapore. He concluded that the RAF's wing of Brewster Buffalos was adequate for the defence of the island. But it was soon found that they were no match for the Japanese Zero, one of the best fighters in the world at the time, which established a kill ratio of 12:1. At the Battle of Midway, US Marine Corps flyers dubbed the Buffalo 'the flying coffin'.

Before the fall of Singapore, Brooke-Popham was relieved, suffering from nervous collapse. But he was not the only one who underestimated the Japanese. Many commanders thought that the Japanese were no match for well-trained British troops. One commander inspecting his men said, 'Don't you think they are worthy of some better enemy than the Japanese?' Another officer said, 'I do hope we are not getting too strong in Malaya, because if so the Japanese may never attempt a landing.'

However, the Japanese had an advantage. On 11 November 1940, the SS *Automedon* was attacked by the German surface raider *Atlantis*, who sank her – but not before removing fifteen bags of top-secret mail prepared by the British War Cabinet's Planning Division and addressed to Brooke-Popham. They contained decoding tables, Fleet orders, gunnery instructions, Naval Intelligence reports, evaluations of the strength of British land and naval forces in the Far East, a detailed report on Singapore's defences, and information on the roles to be played by Australian and New Zealand forces in the Far East in the event that Japan entered the war on the Axis side – which it did thirteen months later.

Singapore had been designed as a fortress against any attack from the sea. But it soon became clear that it was to be attacked from the landward side, after the Japanese landed on the Malay Peninsular. This was because the RAF was being betrayed by Captain Patrick Heenan, who was transmitting their disposition to the Japanese. He was arrested in January 1942 and summarily executed for treason.

With the Japanese at the gates of Singapore, Lieutenant-

General Arthur Percival, who had no combat experience since 1922 and no experience of higher command in war, still refused to build any landward defences on the grounds that 'defences are bad for morale – for both troops and civilians'. Percival was then seen to be in 'a state of dither'. Fearing that water and ammunition were running low, Percival surrendered, although – unknown to him – the Japanese were running out of shells. A garrison of around 120,000 gave up almost without a fight to an invasion force of around a quarter of that number. Winston Churchill called it 'the worst disaster and largest capitulation in British history'.

No good in the air

Since the Iranian Embassy siege in May 1980, Britain's SAS have been seen as the *crème de la crème* of Special Forces who are emulated around the world. But at one time the Special Air Services were no good in the air. The regiment was founded in North Africa 1941 by a young lieutenant named David Stirling. As the battle front moved back and forth along the Mediterranean coast, he looked for a way to hit the enemy in the rear. To put these plans into action, he joined forces with the Australian 'Jock' Lewes, an officer with the Welsh Guards, who scrounged fifty parachutes, and he and Stirling started to make training jumps.

Disaster struck when Stirling's parachute snagged on the tail of the aircraft. Injured in the fall, Stirling spent months in hospital, but this gave him time to do more detailed planning of his new unit. His idea was that a smaller force inserted behind enemy lines could hit lightly guarded targets, disrupting the enemy in the rear.

When he was released from hospital in July, Stirling decided to take his plan to the commander-in-chief in the Middle East, General Sir Claude Auchinleck, but he was refused entry to Auchinleck's headquarters. Even though he was on crutches, he clambered over the perimeter fence and barged into the office of Auchinleck's chief-of-staff Major-General Neil Ritchie. Ritchie was so impressed with the young man's audacity that he presented Stirling's plan to Auchinleck, who quickly saw its virtue. Stirling was promoted captain and ordered to raise a new unit of six officers and sixty men.

Within a week, Stirling had assembled his men at a camp near Kabrit in the Suez Canal Zone. All they had were a few old tents, so the SAS's first operation was a raid on a nearby New Zealanders' camp to purloin new ones. Then they began parachute training by jumping off the back of a Bedford fifteen-hundredweight truck travelling at thirty miles an hour. This caused so many ankle injuries that a proper scaffolding training tower was built. The first time they went up in a plane, they lost two men due to faulty attachment rings. This shook morale, so, the next time they jumped, Stirling was the first man out of the plane.

On 16 November 1941, after a week of planning, the

SAS made its first attack on five enemy airfields around Timimi and Gazala. The unit was to be dropped in teams of twelve, twenty miles from their targets. On the night of the raid, there was a storm. The planes were blown off course. After the drop, none of the teams found their target. On their way to the rendezvous point, they were lashed with rain, then scorched by the sun. Of the sixty-two men sent out, only twenty-two returned. The SAS's first mission against the enemy had been a disaster.

Nevertheless, Stirling managed to persuade Auchinleck that his unit was still viable. But, in future, it would go into action by truck.

Bombing bombed

In the early days of the air offensive against Germany in the Second World War, less than one-third of bombs dropped fell within five miles of their target. Due to equipment failure, enemy action, weather or simply getting lost, only about 5 per cent of the planes that set out got within five miles of their target. On top of that, only 50 per cent of the bombs they dropped actually exploded. In the bombing raids of 1940 and 1941, more British fliers died than German civilians.

Indeed, the British had qualms about bombing civilians, even though the Germans showed no such reserve when it came to bombing the inhabitants of Warsaw, Antwerp and, eventually, British cities. While the Germans thrust into Poland, the RAF confined itself to dropping propaganda leaflets. When a plan to firebomb the Black Forest was suggested, the secretary of state for air, Sir Kingsley Wood, said, 'Are you aware it is private property? Why, you will be asking me to bomb Essen next?'

However, the RAF soon changed its tune when it seemed its budget might be diverted to the army and navy. It came up with a bogus report, which argued that, if the RAF abandoned any attempt at precision bombing and area-bombed cities such as Essen, Duisburg, Düsseldorf and Cologne, 'dehousing' the workforce, it would cripple the German munitions industry, break German morale and win the war.

This became the sole object of Air Marshal Arthur 'Bomber' Harris. He disapproved of the sabotage missions of the Special Operations Executive because, dropping their agents behind enemy lines, diverted his planes from bombing German cities. Air Chief Marshal Charles Portal had moral qualms. 'I think that the dropping of men dressed in civilian clothes for the purpose of attempting to kill members of the opposing forces is not an operation with which the Royal Air Force should be associated,' he said. They were overruled. Air Marshal Harris also had to be ordered to divert his plane to bomb the railways and military targets in France in the run-up to the D-Day landings.

The debate about the effectiveness of area bombing in Europe in the Second World War continues to this day. According to the US Strategic Bombing Survey conducted after the war, bombing had very little effect on German armaments production or on the German people's general commitment to the war. In fact, the targeting of civilians had the reverse effect, actually strengthening the will of the German people. Meanwhile, RAF Bomber Command lost 55,000 young men; the US Eighth Army Air Force 105,000; and between 305,000 and 600,000 German civilians perished.

CHAPTER ELEVEN

Uniformed Failures

IN THE PAST, UNIFORMS HAVE been as much of a hindrance as a help to English armies. The white bands across red tunics favoured in the eighteenth and nineteenth centuries helped snipers aiming for the heart. Even after they had learnt their lesson and opted for a muted khaki, white arm bands the British at Gallipoli wore for identification at night helped the Turks pick them off.

'We shall know better . . . another time'

The British were slow to learn that the cumbersome uniforms worn on European battlefields were not suited to war in the Americas. This was a lesson the French learnt early on. When the French and Indian War broke out in 1754, the French ditched their clumsy livery and adopted Indian-style dress and moccasins. They also realised that the wooded terrain of North America did not suit European-style set-piece battles, so concentrated on the cowardly tactics of taking cover behind trees and laying ambushes.

General Edward Braddock, commander of the British expedition to North America, would have none of it. Standards of gentlemanly behaviour had to be maintained. An officer in the Coldstream Guards, he had attended to administrative assignments during the War of the Austrian Succession, later serving as governor of Gibraltar. Although he had no experience in the field, he had friends at court, and Prince William Augustus, the Duke of Cumberland, had secured him the command in North America. His first task was to seize Fort Duquesne, the site of modern Pittsburgh, and drive the French back into Canada. To get there, Braddock decided to build a road, bridging every creek. This slowed his advance and gave the French plenty of warning that he was coming. It also consigned his men to months in the great dark forests of Ohio, where they swapped stories of the unimaginable cruelty of the savages they saw lurking behind every tree.

Outnumbered, the French decided not to wait in the fort for the British to arrive, but to go out and ambush them. Braddock realised this and sent out an advance guard under Colonel Gage to spring any trap that awaited them. Gage came upon a man dressed like an Indian, but with a telltale French collar piece. This was Captain Beaujeu, the French commander. Beaujeu quickly dispersed his men among the trees. Meanwhile, Gage did the gentlemanly thing and drew his redcoats up into lines for battle. They were shot down by the unseen enemy. A cannon fired into the undergrowth was no help.

While the way ahead was blocked by the French, the Indians ran down the flanks, making blood-curdling war cries that put the fear of God into the British column. Caught in the crossfire, the advance guard retreated on to the rear guard who, by mistake, began shooting them. As Braddock rode around trying to rally his men, four horses were shot from under him. Still having not learnt his lesson, he ordered his men to form up into ranks as if on a parade ground, only to have them shot down. When Braddock saw some of his redcoats taking cover behind a fallen tree, he chased them out at the point of a sabre. They had been ordered to take cover there by a young Virginian officer who knew more about fighting in American conditions than Braddock. His name was George Washington.

To identify himself as the commanding officer, Braddock had tied a white handkerchief around this hat. This was a gift for a marksman. Eventually, he was shot through the chest, possibly by one of his own men.

Two-thirds of his men had been killed or wounded, including sixty out of the eighty-six officers. As Braddock lay dying, he told Washington, 'We shall better know how to deal with them another time.' They didn't. However, in proper eighteenth-century style, Braddock left his fortune to an actress.

If at first you don't succeed . . .

One of Braddock's successors in North America was Major-General James Abercromby. Formerly the king's painter in Scotland, he had been a quartermaster in the Royal Scots. Fat, lazy and lacking in ambition, on his one foray into the field he had been wounded. Nevertheless, he gained command in North America, thanks to the patronage of the Duke of Newcastle and the Earl of Loudoun. In March 1758, William Pitt ordered Abercromby to take Fort Ticonderoga with the Royal American regiment, who wore red coats like their British counterparts. He advanced with sixteen thousand men. The fort was held by just 3,600 men under the command of Luis Joseph, Marquis de Montcalm.

Montcalm cut down all the trees in front of the fort to build a breastwork nine feet high. When Abercromby arrived he rejected the wisest course – to mount cannons on the top of Mount Defiance that dominated the fort, and bombard it. The guns would be left in the boats. He also discarded the ungentlemanly option of attacking the fort from the weaker sides or rear. Instead, he ordered his redcoats to form up and advance in ranks in a frontal assault through the tangle of trees and branches the French had laid down. Meanwhile, he remained two miles to the rear while his men were massacred by the French shooting through loopholes. Those who reached the front wall and tried to climb it were bayoneted or knocked off. This went on for five hours while Abercromby repeatedly ordered them to advance and attack. The British had suffered more than two thousand casualties before they were forced to retreat.

Despite his staggering incompetence, Abercromby was promoted lieutenant-general in 1772. His son was killed at Bunker Hill.

. . . Try, try again

By 1815, the Americans were facing the British troops who had defeated Napoleon. But they were still wearing those damned red coats. At the Battle of New Orleans, they were commanded by Sir Edward Pakenham, Wellington's brother-in-law, who had seen action in the Peninsular War. 'Pakenham may not be the brightest genius, but my partiality for him does not lead me astray when I tell you that he is one of the best we have,' Wellington wrote in dispatches. Well, even Wellington had to keep in with his wife. Rejecting Pakenham's marriage proposal in 1812, Annabella Milbanke said, 'All the Pakenham family have a strong tendency to insanity.' Instead she married Byron.

The troops under his command were not happy about their duties in the New World. After fighting for Wellington for seven years, they assumed they were to be sent back to Britain to be discharged. Instead, they found themselves sailing into the Gulf of Mexico, then dumped in the swamps of Louisiana. Tempers were not improved when the troops had to carry cannonballs up to the front in their knapsacks. The whole thing was futile, as the war had been ended by the Treaty of Ghent signed on 24 December 1814. However, the news had not got through to Pakenham or the American General Andrew Jackson.

Jackson had some five thousand men. Some had been regulars or militiamen, but most were civilian volunteers, pirates, freebooters and freed slaves. In formal combat, they would have stood no chance. But Jackson put his men behind earthworks and a barricade of cotton bales with a swamp at one end and a river at the other. If the British were foolish enough to attack, they had to make a frontal assault.

And that's exactly what Pakenham ordered his men to do. Even in the gloom of the bayous, their conspicuous red coats stood out as they marched towards the camouflaged rebels with fixed bayonets. When the front rank was cut down by musket fire, Pakenham decided to lead the second rank into action. He was shot down along with his men. The British suffered more than two thousand casualties; the Americans seventy-one.

Hessians sacked

During the American War of Independence, the American soldiers were informally dressed, while the British persisted in wearing the red tunics adopted by the Parliamentarian army during the Civil War. Meanwhile, Britain's Hessian mercenaries insisted on maintaining the highest European sartorial standards. They wore breeches that were so tight that it was impossible to bend down to dodge a bullet, while a thick leather collar made it impossible to duck. And the silver badges they wore on their hats invited the Americans to aim for the brain.

However, they always appeared alert. They wore pigtails that drew their hair back so tightly that they could not close their eyes. But that did not mean they were awake. Regulations stipulated the number of locks that were to be visible either side. So, the day before a battle, men would stay up all night doing their hair. Such attention to detail was thought to be vital for discipline.

Boots, boots, boots, boots . . .

In 1914, Rudyard Kipling wrote the poem 'Boots', emphasising the importance of hobnails in the imperial project. Just sixty years before, in the Crimean War, the British Army had been let down badly by their footwear.

Economies at the War Department meant that soles dropped off British Army boots after a week's wear. On one occasion, the 55th (Westmorland) Regiment of Foot sank into a sea of mud when they were on parade. When they pulled their boots out, they left the soles behind, leaving the men to go into action in stockinged feet.

Boots were also supplied in standard sizes. But, in the bitter cold, men needed to wear two pairs of socks. And, in the damp, their feet swelled up, making it impossible to get their boots on. More were sent on the supply ship *Prince*, but it sank. British troops took to stealing boots off the corpses of their allies, the Turks, and their enemies, the Russians. When Midshipman Evelyn Wood's boots gave out, he gave a sailor ten shillings to dig up a pair of Russian boots from the graves along Inkerman Ridge.

Crimean couture

Along with inadequate boots, soldiers in the Crimea also lacked proper uniforms. When troops first landed in September 1854, they were told to leave their knapsacks containing a spare set of clothing on the transports. These promptly sailed, leaving the men with only the clothes they stood up in. When the transports returned six weeks later, the knapsacks had been ransacked.

In the wet weather, men had to fight on day after day in the same sodden uniforms. The seams rotted and they fell apart. Greatcoats were at a premium. Forty-thousand also went down on board the *Prince*. Another twelve thousand arrived safely in November, but only three thousand were issued, as Army Regulations maintained that a man could be issued a greatcoat only once every three years. Any man who had lost his coat during the fighting faced freezing to death, while nine thousand warm coats remained in store.

Then, at the height of summer, soldiers were dressed in their thick winter uniforms. At Sevastopol, General Sir George

Brown insisted that the Light Division wear high-buttoned collars and stocks, white material tied like a cravat and worn as a part of formal horse-riding dress in the eighteenth century.

The coming of khaki

After the Boer War, the British had the good sense to abandon the traditional red coat, adopted by the Parliamentarian army in 1645, and kit out their men in the considerably less conspicuous khaki. For two centuries the German infantry had worn dark Prussian-blue uniforms. By the First World War, these were replaced by field grey. But the French persisted in dressing their soldiers in red and blue.

Before the war, the French minister for war, Adolphe Méssimy, had the temerity to suggest that the soldiers of the Third Republic wear a more muted battledress. This was greeted with consternation. The cry went up, '*Le pantaloon rouge, c'est la France*' – 'The red trouser, it is France.'

Méssimy was replaced in 1914 and was wounded while commanding an infantry battalion the following year.

The French even kept their traditional red kepi, mocking the German spiked *pickelhaube*, even though – as a metal helmet – it saved a lot of lives. At the First Battle of the Marne in September, the 246th Infantry Regiment stood out against the light-yellow wheat fields so well in sunlight that the Germans were a mile away dazzled. Just in case the enemy had missed them, they unfurled the regimental colours and struck up the band. They were annihilated. Unfortunately, it seems, they were not quite so visible to their own side and survivors of the enemy onslaught were fired on by their own artillery.

Nevertheless, the Spahis and the Zouaves, elite regiments from North Africa, continued wearing bright clothing. They also maintained six regiments of Cuirassiers, dressed – like English horse guards – with shiny breastplates and helmets with long horsehair plumes to make them an easy target.

On the other side, Austrian horsemen wore yellow breeches and their officers wore a yellow sash. In the first four months of the war, a third of the officers in the Austro-Hungarian army were killed or wounded – nearly eleven thousand in all.

Khaki, or a variation of it, is now almost universal for battledress, although it now usually comes in DPM – Disruptive Pattern Material.

CHAPTER TWELVE

Suspect Supplies

HE SOLDIERS AND SAILORS WHO fight beastly battles are often treated beastily. Their rations are inedible, their clothing inadequate and the conditions they are expected to live and fight in unsustainable. Consequently, they are prone to disease, ill health, suffering and death, even when they are far from the battlefield. In Old England, more men died due to their treatment by the own side than ever died at the hands of the enemy.

Rum, bum and concertina

Sailors were often kept short of water. Fresh water was a bulky commodity to carry on board ship. Algae grew in the casks and the water became slimy. And drinking sea-water dehydrates you further, which can drive you crazy. But there was always the rum ration. After the conquest of Jamaica in 1655, British sailors were given half a pint of rum a day, instead of French brandy. Some saved it up and drank

261

it all at once, causing disciplinary problems. So, in 1740, Admiral Edward Vernon ordered that the rum be diluted. Lime or lemon juice was added to disguise the taste of the stagnant water. It was soon noted that Vernon's sailors were healthier than others. In 1747 James Lind formally demonstrated that citrus fruits such as lime and lemon prevented scurvy, and the rest of the navy took up issuing 'grog'. The name came from Vernon's nickname, 'Old Grog', given to him because the coat he habitually wore was made of grogram, a fabric made of silk mixed with wool or mohair and stiffened with gum.

From 1756, British sailors were given half a pint of rum mixed with a quart of water in two servings, one before noon, the other at the end of the working day. The practice was ended in the US Navy in 1862, but the Royal Navy continued giving its rum ration, though it had been halved in 1850. It was stopped for officers in 1881 and for warrant officers in 1918. Then, in 1970, it was ended for ratings too when it was finally decided that, in modern ships, it was best to keep the sailors more or less sober. Men were given an extra can of beer in compensation. However, in the eighteenth and nineteenth centuries, life on board sailing ships was so harsh that it was better to keep the men half-drunk.

Ward's pills and drops

Commodore George Anson was compared to Francis Drake after his round-the-world voyage during the War of Jenkins' Ear (1739–48) netted more than half a million pounds in plunder. However, rather than trust in citrus fruits, already suspected of being an effective protection against scurvy, he put his faith in the pills and drops of 'Doctor' Joshua Ward, a notorious quack who claimed his remedy would cure everything from syphilis to cancer. Of the 1,955 men who set out on the voyage, 60 per cent failed to return.

Admittedly, many of them were not in the best of health to start with. Thirty-two were taken from the hospital in Gosport. Another five hundred were Chelsea Pensioners. Old and infirm, they were expected to walk to Portsmouth. Only 260 arrived – with the younger and fitter men seizing the opportunity to desert.

Delays meant that the squadron set off in September, which meant that the journey to Madeira took forty days rather than the twelve it took in more favourable seasons. By the time they set out across the Atlantic, the provisions were already mouldy. Typhus – 'ship's fever' – was spread through the crew by the body lice that thrived in humid and unsanitary conditions below deck. Then an epidemic of 'fluxes' – dysentery – spread through the entire comple-ment. In just two months, 120 men had died on Anson's flagship, HMS *Centurion*, alone. Another eighty were so ill that they had to be left in Brazil. A further twenty-eight died of malaria while they were in port.

Back on board, the symptoms of scurvy began to appear – swollen and bleeding gums, loose teeth, stiff and sore joints and bleeding beneath the skin and in deep tissue. Wounds became slow to heal and the men suffered the effects of anaemia. Their teeth fell out and their gums were so sore that it was impossible to eat. (One man who was injured at the Battle of the Boyne in 1690 found that his wounds reopened fifty years later.)

The squadron managed to reach Cape Horn in March, the beginning of the stormy season, which did little to improve their condition. Hundreds of men died as they battled their way around the Horn. The storms were so severe that the *Severn* turned back. By the time it reached Rio on 6 June, 158 of the crew were dead. Another 114 were so sick they were of little use, leaving just thirty men and boys to sail the ship. The *Gloucester* had only one fit officer, while the sloop *Trial* had three men and two officers fit for duty to sail her. The pursuer wrote that the 'weather was still stormy with huge deep, hollow seas that frequently broke quite over us, with constant rain, frost or snow. Our decks were always full of water, and our men constantly falling ill with the scurvy; and the allowance of water being but small reduced us to a most deplorable condition.'

Reaching Selkirk's Island off the coast of Chile – where the real-life Robinson Crusoe had been stranded – the ill were sent ashore, though there were 'at least a dozen who died in the boats on their being exposed to the fresh air', according to the official account. But the survivors found turnips and radishes growing on the island and their condition improved. Abandoning his reliance on Ward's pills and drops, Anson himself planted lettuces, carrots, plums, peaches and apricots.

In a head count on leaving the island, only 335 of the 961 who had sailed on the *Centurion, Gloucester* and *Trial* were found to be still alive. The *Pearl* had also turned back, while the *Wager*, under her third captain since leaving Portsmouth – and he was ill – had sunk. A hundred and forty men made it ashore. Variously starved, drowned, imprisoned and enslaved, only thirty-six of those men from the *Wager* made it back to England.

Anson took £18,000 of bullion from the *Nuestra Señora del Monte Carmelo* off Panama and another £5,000 in silver from the *Arranzazu* outside Valparasio. More prizes were seized up and down the coast of South America. Finally, the treasure ship *Covadonga*, carrying 1,313,843 pieces of eight and 35,682 ounces of silver, was taken before the squadron headed across the Pacific and then back to England.

Of the 510 men who set out on board Anson's flagship *Centurion*, only 130 returned. From the *Covadonga* alone, Anson made an estimated £91,000, worth some £664 million at today's prices. He went on to become first lord of the Admiralty.

Taking the biscuit

In 1824, Colonel Sir Charles M'Carthy was governor of Sierra Leone and sided with the Fante against the Ashante and sent out a small force. When they met ten thousand Ashante, M'Carthy ordered the band to strike up 'God Save the King' in the hope that some disaffected Ashante might defect. They responded with war drums.

His redcoats then formed a square in an attempt to hold

off the Ashante. Soon they were running low on ammunition. But, when M'Carthy ordered new boxes to be opened, it was found that they were full of biscuits. Almost all the British force were killed. M'Carthy's heart was eaten by the principal Ashante chief. His jawbone was used as drum sticks and his skull was gold-rimmed and used as a drinking-cup by Ashante rulers, though it was later returned to England.

Ironically, this heroic servant of empire was not an Englishman at all. He was born Charles Guéroult, the second son of Frenchman Jean Gabriel Guéroult. His mother was the granddaughter of Charles Thaddeus François MacCarthy, one of the original Irish 'Wild Geese' who fled to France with James II. Guéroult changed his name and joined the French Irish Brigade. After the French Revolution, the Irish Brigade was reorganised under British pay. M'Carthy then worked his way up through the army to become a knight and a colonial governor.

Battle of the booze

In British India, the officers enjoyed a gay round of social and sporting events. But for the other ranks there was little to do but drink. In 1835, for example, the 674 customers of the 49th Regiment's canteen drank 7,217 gallons of *arrack* – a strong rice liquor distilled locally – 177 of brandy and 144 of gin. There were frequent deaths from alcoholism.

Sea food

Sailors survived on salt beef and hard tack, but were given much less than the four thousand calories a day needed by a man doing heavy manual labour. Generally, they assumed that the salt beef was horse – and old ''oss' at that. Salt beef found in the stores on Ascension Island in 1839 was found to have been preserved in 1809. It was still edible, but best served boiled and grated. While ''oss' served up in the 1870s had been salted while Nelson was still alive. It was so tough that one sailor carved a model frigate out of it. Sanded and varnished and mounted, it was as hard as mahogany.

On board ship there was very little opportunity for foraging, but the enterprising Sir Sidney Smith would drop a baited fishing line into the hold and angle for rats. Cooked, they were as tasty as duck, he insisted.

The hard tack – ship's biscuit – was more nutritious, but because of the maggots and weevils that infested it. Sailors used to leave a fish on the top of a sack of hard tack to attract all the maggots into it, then throw it away. However, it may have been more nutritious to have eaten the fish and thrown out the biscuit.

Salt beef and hard tack are certainly not what you want to eat if you are suffering from scurvy and have sore and bleeding gums, and teeth that are falling out.

Water, water, everywhere . . .

In 1845, HMS *America* was under the command of Captain Gordon, brother of the prime minister, the Earl of Aberdeen.

She became becalmed off the coast of South America and the water ration was reduced to half a pint a day – that is, for the men. The chicken and other livestock kept to supply the captain's table got more. One petty officer was broken down to able seaman for trying to collect moisture using a sponge. Ordinary seamen were flogged for drinking the captain's bathwater, which you would have thought was punishment enough.

Thirsty men who succumbed to drinking seawater went mad. One who tried stretching his ration with vinegar died. The captain even refused the help of natives, who offered them supplies. When he returned to England prematurely, he was reprimanded for leaving his post without permission, but the matter of the crew's water was never mentioned.

Supplies, supplies

During the Crimean War, British troops got smaller rations than the convicts. An inmate of a Scottish prison would get 25.16 ounces (713 grams) of food a day, including milk, fish, bread and vegetables. A British soldier got 23.52 ounces (667 grams) of food, according the army commissioners sent out there to investigate, compared with 28.5 ounces (808 grams) for a British sailor or a massive 32.96 ounces (934 grams) for a Hessian mercenary. On Christmas Day 1854, Colonel Bell's men got no rations at all. 'I kicked up a dust,' Bell wrote in his diary. 'At the close of the day the Commissary did serve out a small portion of fresh meat. Too late! no fires, or means of cooking!' When the food was issued, the men were too exhausted to collect it. All they were interested in was coffee and the rum ration.

Under Queen's Regulations each soldier should have received 1½ pounds (680 grams) of leaven bread or 1 pound of biscuit and 1 pound (454 grams) of fresh or salt meat a day. For this his pay was stopped 3½d (that is, old pennies = 1.5 new pence). Anything else he needed he was expected to buy. Lord Raglan recognised that this system was unworkable in Turkey and the Crimea and had ordered that, for the stoppage of a further penny (0.42 pence), each soldier should receive an ounce (28.35 grams) of coffee and 1¾ ounces (50 grams) of sugar. Later on he ordered that 2 ounces (56.7 grams) of rice or barley should be added to the daily ration, an extra half-pound (227 grams) of meat and a free issue of a quarter of a pint of spirits. But transport difficulties had made it impossible to get these rations up to the men.

For three or four days at a time, they had nothing to eat but biscuit. The fresh meat that came up perhaps once in ten days was seldom edible. Besides, the commissariat found it more difficult to issue than salt beef. However, the salt beef caused diarrhoea. It was impossible to boil the salt out of it because the camp kettles had been discarded during the march to the Alma River and mess tins did not hold enough water. Consequently, men threw the meat away, preferring to survive on rum and biscuits alone.

Scurvy on shore

It had been known for a hundred years that going without fresh fruit or vegetables – or even bread and fresh meat – caused scurvy. But the disease was rampant among the British soldiers in the Crimea. On 4 November 1854, the *Harbinger* arrived with 150 tons of vegetables on board. However, it had left the Bosphorus without the right papers and, consequently, could not be unloaded. Eventually, the cargo was either stolen by marauding bands of Zouaves or went rotten and had to be thrown overboard. None got to the men at the front.

The following month, three steamers arrived loaded with vegetables. Much of the cargo was already rotten. There was no means of getting the rest up to the camps and another £3,000 worth of vegetables were dumped in the sea. On another occasion a commissariat officer refused to accept a cargo of fresh vegetables, as he 'had no power to purchase them'. The men were reduced to a ration of two potatoes and one onion a month. The gums of men suffering from scurvy were sore and bleeding, and, like sailors, they found eating the hard biscuit painful.

On 19 December 20,000 pounds (9,000kg) of lime juice arrived, but it was not until Lord Raglan called for an inventory of the goods in store that anyone in authority seemed aware of its arrival. On 29 January, he ordered that lime juice should form part of the soldiers' ration. But even this presented difficulties of transportation. However, he forgot to renew the order for rice to be sent to the troops to ease their bowel disorders.

Dr Blake, surgeon of the 55th, recorded that he treated a total of 3,025 cases of sickness compared with 564 men treated for wounds; and his regiment was one of those most heavily engaged at Inkerman.

Green coffee

Unroasted coffee beans were shipped in, because they were less prone to dampness and mould on the journey. But there was no immediate means to hand for roasting and grinding them, and the foul concoction they made was undrinkable if not actually harmful.

'A ration of green raw coffee was served out, a mockery in the midst of all this misery,' wrote one officer. 'Nothing to roast coffee, nothing to grind it, no fire, no sugar; and unless it was meant that we eat it as horses do barley, I don't see what use the men could make of it, except what they have just done, pitched it into the mud!'

However, more enterprising Tommies began to cut up their salt beef or discarded boots to make fuel to roast the coffee beans. And cannonballs and shell casings were then used to grind them.

Thanks to another bureaucratic snafu at the commissariat, there were 2,075 pounds of tea in the stores that were never issued.

French leave

The French were much better provisioned. They had set up bakeries in Balaclava, but the ordinary British soldier did not have the money to buy fresh bread. An English artillery officer, who had previously not 'reckoned much to them', now thought the French 'splendid fellows; opinions had entirely changed'. Another officer said that they were 'a very civil lot'. Although their camps were considered filthy, they had canteens where, in the evening, brandy and wine were served by pretty *vivandières*. This was the greatest pleasure that life could then afford, said one.

Of course, the British had to pay for their pleasures. Lieutenant Stacpoole complained to his brother that he was charged five francs 'for the very worst *vin ordinaire* that you could get for six sous in Paris'. A small loaf of brown bread baked daily in the French army's ovens cost five shillings (25 pence) – £17 at today's prices.

Most French soldiers were expert chefs, making gourmet meals from the most unpromising ingredients – from tortoises, even from rats, which they would ask permission to catch in Balaclava and take back to their camps impaled on long sticks.

The Zouaves were the most admired for culinary audacity. It is thought they stole Lord Rokeby's patent water closet to make soup in. The whole British army was delighted at the news.

Palliasses

British soldiers slept shrouded by sodden greatcoats or a single blanket on the muddy floor of their tents. Palliasses (straw mattresses) had been supplied but, as there was no hay or straw in the Crimea to stuff them with, none were issued. Thanks to some mix-up, 25,000 rugs arrived in January 1855. They were a perfect substitute for blankets or palliasses to keep out the cold and damp. But just eight hundred were issued, despite the appalling conditions. It seems that Army Regulations were deter-

mined to strangle British soldiers with red tape. This was even recognised by Colonel Alexander Tulloch and Sir John McNeill, who were sent out to investigate the shortcomings of the commissariat in 1855. Their report concluded that 'deaths . . . amount to about 35 per cent of the average strength of the army present in the Crimea from 1 October 1854 to 30 April 1855 . . . this excessive mortality is not to be attributed to anything peculiarly unfavourable in the climate, but to overwork, exposure to wet and cold, improper food, insufficient clothing during part of the winter and insufficient shelter from the inclement weather.'

The commissariat was reformed by Royal Warrant in 1858, two years after the end of the war.

Things were, of course, different for the top brass. While Lord Lucan billeted with his troops, his brother-in-law Lord Cardigan lived aboard his luxurious yacht moored in the Black Sea.

A Nightingale sang

Even the French sick and wounded were better off than the ordinary Tommy. They were given good bread, peas and beans, rice, dandelions, coffee, sugar and 'bellyfuls of warm soup'. While the English shivered in the cold, the French – both the sick and the well – were kept warm with sheepskins. Captain Robert Portal noted that at the French Army field hospital at Kamiesch 'they have erected long huts and made quite a village . . . The wounded are carefully laid on beds in rows, then come the sick and so on; everything clean and nice; the man's name and complaint on a piece of paper over his bed, as if he was in a barrack hospital. Then they have huts in which all the medicines are arranged and everything got at, at a moment's notice. Then again, close to the hospital huts, are large cooking huts where soup is constantly made.'

Meanwhile, at Scutari, when Florence Nightingale took charge, she found men lying on the floor in what was little more than an open sewer with no blankets or pillows. And, when the *Prince* sank, it took with it the army's supply of opium, quinine, ammonia and other important drugs.

'There were no vessels for water or utensils of any kind; no soap, towels, or clothes, no hospital clothes,' she wrote, 'the men lying in their uniforms, stiff with gore and covered with filth to a degree and of a kind no one could write about; their persons covered with vermin.'

A chaplain who visited to comfort the wounded found himself instantly infested with lice.

At any one time there were a thousand men suffering

from dysentery with only twenty chamber pots to go around – and there was no running water to wash them out. A visit to the latrine meant wading through sewage. Barrels were put in the wards, but that only made the air there stink.

'I shall never forget the sights as long as I live,' wrote another nurse, named Elizabeth Davis. The superintendent of her party, a sister of the Sellonites order, told her not to speak to the patients. But she could not resist asking the first man she attended how he was, whereupon the superintendent 'scolded me for doing so, and repeated her order that I should not speak to them. I began to open some of their wounds. The first that I touched was a case of frost bite. The toes of both the man's feet fell off with the bandages. The hand of another fell off at the wrist. It was a fortnight, or from that to six weeks, since the wounds of many of those men had been looked at and dressed . . . One soldier had been wounded at Alma. His wound had not been dressed for five weeks, and I took at least a quart of maggots from it. From many of the other patients I removed them in hand-fuls.'

The lack of food did not help.

'We have not seen a drop of milk, and the bread is extremely sour,' wrote Nightingale. 'The butter is most filthy; it is Irish butter in a state of decomposition; and the meat is more like moist leather than food. Potatoes we are waiting for, until they arrive from France.'

The best she could do was put up screens to prevent the patients watching others undergo gruesome operations. But nothing could stifle their screams.

On the battlefield things were even worse. After the

battle of Alma in September 1894, the surgeon George Lawson wrote:

> On the 20th, when the Light Division had about 1,000 killed or wounded, there were no ambulances, etc., or lights (save the personal property of the officers) – nearly all of the operations requiring to be performed on the ground. I, myself, operated the whole of the first day on the poor fellows on the ground, and had performed many on the second, until an old door was discovered, of which we made a table.

Amputated limbs were stacked up outside the hospital, where they were eaten by pigs, or seen floating in the harbour at Balaclava.

Horse meat

One of the problems the British had with supply in the Crimea was transportation. The Royal Horse Artillery had to hand over their prized steeds to the commissariat. But undernourishment took its toll and soon they were pitifully weak. 'My teams would disgrace a pedlar,' Captain Shakespear wrote to his mother.

Fresh packhorses sent over from Constantinople had arrived on 2 December but by 5 January they could be seen dying every day. On the track from Balaclava, horse after horse sank down into the mud and died, leaving the cart stranded. As soon as the British driver went off for help, enterprising Zouaves or starving Turks would make off with the

abandoned cargo. They would steal the cart for firewood, skin the horse and strip the carcass of its meat. When the British driver returned, he would find the rims of the wheels and a few bones lying in the snow or mud.

Lost and far from home

In the Crimean War, the British Army were also short of maps, so one officer wrote home to his mother, 'Will you also be kind enough to send me a map of the Crimea with forts, etc., well marked out in Sebastopol. I see them advertised at Wylds in the Strand. You can choose which you think best and send it by post.'

Fight! Fight! Fight!

During an attack on the Redan at Sevastopol, the 18th Regiment crossed a cemetery and took shelter in some outlying houses, which they were surprised to find were occupied by Russian women and children. After the soldiers reassured them that they would not be harmed, the women made them some coffee, which was much appreciated. The men then got out their rations, which they ate off the covers of fine books they had found in the houses.

They then found some wine and got so drunk that they were later seen swaggering around in women's dresses and bonnets. Then things turned unpleasant. A fight started between two soldiers over a looted item. They slugged it out in a makeshift ring formed by the rest of the regiment as the battle raged around them. They did not hear that the assault had been a failure until after nightfall. Largely unscathed, they returned carrying drunken comrades on doors they had ripped from the houses.

Pay day

The soldiers who fight beastly battles are seldom well paid. But sometimes they get lucky.

In 1885, a column of eleven hundred men was sent to relieve General Gordon, who was under siege at Khartoum. On 17 January, it came under attack by a force of twelve thousand Dervishes under the Mahdi, the title of the last imam before the end of the world. Although heavily outnumbered, the British were confident of victory because they had one of the early machine guns that had just been introduced. In Britain it had been tested thoroughly and found to be reliable. However, it had not been tried in desert conditions. Sand got into the mechanism and, after seventy rounds, it jammed.

The Dervishes were then able to do the unthinkable – they broke the British square. In the midst of the battle, the British opened their reserve ammunition boxes, only to find them full of gold sovereigns, which were to be used to buy off vacillating tribesmen. Despite the oncoming Dervishes, the men took time to stuff their pockets.

This lucrative distraction does not seem to have affected

the outcome of the battle. The British claimed a victory with casualties of 158 against the Dervishes' 1,100. However, only half the Dervish force had been engaged. The column arrived too late to save Gordon. Sudan was ruled by the Dervishes for the next thirteen years until an Anglo-Egyptian force under Kitchener invaded again in 1898.

About the Author

NIGEL CAWTHORNE HAS BEEN an author for over thirty years. He has written on subjects as diverse as history, crime, sex, war and fashion. He is the author of the bestselling *Sex Lives of ...* series, including (in rather dubious taste) *Sex Lives of the Popes*. Nigel lives in London, and can usually be found in the British Library.